SILENCE NOT
A LOVE STORY

Also By Cynthia L. Cooper

Plays
How She Played the Game
Slow Burn
Strange Light
Sisters of Sisters
Beyond Stone
The Outermost House
Go, Girl, Go
Sentences and Words
Strange Bedfellows
Works of Art
The Dwelling Place
Intervention
Sor Juana
Saving Grace
Dirty Laundry
Braille: The World at Your Finger Tips (co-author)

Nonfiction
Mockery of Justice (Penguin)
Who Said It Would Be Easy (co-author, Liz Holtzman) (Arcade)

SILENCE NOT
A LOVE STORY

Written by
Cynthia L. Cooper

GIHON RIVER PRESS
East Stroudsburg, PA

Copyright © 2009 by Cynthia L. Cooper

Published by
Gihon River Press
P.O. Box 88
East Stroudsburg PA, 18301
www.gihonriverpress.com

Cover and text design by: A Good Thing Inc.
Front Cover Photo: Steve Feuer

All rights reserved. Published in the United States of America.

No part of this book may be used or reproduced in any manner whatsoever without the written permission of the publisher.

CAUTION: Professionals and amateurs are hereby warned that the play in this book is subject to a royalty for performance. The play is fully protected under copyright laws of the United States of America, and of all countries covered by the International Copyright Union (including the Dominion of Canada and the rest of the British Commonwealth), and all countries covered by the Pan-American Copyright convention and Universal Copyright conventions, and all countries with which the United States has reciprocal copyright relations. All rights, including professional, amateur, motion picture, recitation, lecturing, public reading radio broadcasting, television, video or sound taping, digital recording or delivery and all other forms of mechanical, electronic or digital reproductions such as CD-ROM and CD-I, information developed in the future and the rights of translation into foreign languages, are strictly reserved. Particular emphasis is laid upon the question of public reading, permission for which must be secured from the author Cynthia L. Cooper in writing. For further information, contact the author at plays@cyncooperwriter.net or www.cyncooperwriter.net

DISCLAIMER: The publisher has made every reasonable effort to identify rights holders to any intellectual property contained in this book in order to obtain permissions and give proper credit. If you feel you own the rights to any intellectual property that is contained in this book but have not given your permission for its inclusion, please contact the publisher who will correct the situation for the next printing.

First Edition

10 9 8 7 6 5 4 3 2 1

ISBN 978-0-9819906-0-6

Library of Congress Cataloging-in-Publication

Table of Contents

Acknowledgements	vii
Introduction	1
Prologue: The World of the Play	3
Cast of Characters	9
Silence Not A Love Story—the play	15
Photo Section	
Time line of the period	115
Postscript	119
Where to find more information and bibliography	129

Acknowledgements

Many people helped with the research, development and preparation of this material. My special thanks to: Jennifer Clarke, Dr. Marilyn Frost, Minnesota Supreme Court Justice Rosalie Wahl (Ret.), Rusty and Burt Cohen, Lyn Date, Steve Feuer and Gihon River Press, German Resistance Memorial Center (Berlin), the Konopka Institute for Best Practices in Adolescent Health at the University of Minnesota Division of General Pediatrics and Adolescent Health, Lotte Kohler, Milt Adams and Beaver's Pond, Angelica Torn and the Geraldine Page Center for the Arts, Carolyn Levy and Hamline University Theater Department, Maureen McNeil and The Anne Frank Center USA, Steve Coats, Michael angel Johnson, Susann Brinkley, Wright On! Playwrights, Kitty Chen, Lory Frankel, Lisa Lindstrom, Joanne Edelmann, Elizabeth Holtzman, Jennifer Lyons, Judy Williams and James Lader.

Introduction to Silence Not A Love Story

By Elizabeth Holtzman

Gisa Peiper, a young woman who joins the anti-Nazi resistance in Germany before the Nazis take power and persists in her activities for three years after they take over, seems astonishing to us. She has taken on a force of extraordinary evil and power, and her daring and defiance seem almost incomprehensible. Is she strong and courageous--or quixotic, naive, reckless ... even mad?

Challenging forces of evil, however, is not a phenomenon so remote from our lives as to leave us uncomprehending or indifferent. There have been people in our own time and in our own midst who also stood up to terrible injustice. Take the civil rights movement. Less than fifty years ago, young people, mostly black, challenged the "Jim Crow" system of segregation in the South. They sat in at lunch counters where blacks were excluded and patiently waited to be served; they tried to enter libraries, swimming pools, movies theaters, and bus terminals from which blacks were barred, seeking to be admitted. Sometimes they simply marched peaceably with signs calling for the right to vote. They were met with ferocious hostility—spitting and jeering crowds of angry whites. The entire apparatus of law enforcement turned against them with snarling dogs, cattle prods, water hoses, illegal arrests, illegal beatings, segregated juries, segregated courthouses, and judges with segregated minds. In the end, the assassination of three young civil rights workers, two white and one black, in Mississippi in 1964 finally shocked America into realizing that segregation was not some quaint regional affectation, but rather a horrendous and malevolent institution that had to be ended. And it was.

When the activists started they did not know what the outcome would be. How could they? How could Rosa Parks, who refused to move to the back of the bus in Montgomery, Alabama, have any idea that her simple act would trigger a citywide boycott, end the segregation of buses in Montgomery, and, ultimately, in its widening arcs, shatter Jim Crow across the entire South. Indeed, what rational mind looking at a system of segregation that had been entrenched for more than three hundred years, ever since black people were first brought to the U.S. shores as slaves, could believe that modest acts of moral confrontation could, like blasts from Joshua's trumpet, bring down the walls of such a system? Yet, those who participated had an amazing faith that their actions could bring change—that by confronting evil peaceably, they would persuade others to join or at least to see the justice of their cause. And while our heroine, Gisa Peiper, and her comrades were unable to stop the onslaught of the Nazis in Germany, others like her who engaged in acts of resistance in another age and another place, did end the system of Jim Crow.

For the heroine of this play, Gisa Peiper, and for Rosa Parks and the civil rights activists, their very humanity lay in their acts of resisting evil. They could no more remain passive, removed, and quiescent than they could stop breathing. Whether their actions would work or make a difference was unknown to them. But they knew that they had to act. Out of a deep inner urgency, they had to do something—anything—to stop the evil.

Plato said that the unexamined life was not worth living. For Gisa Peiper and for the civil rights workers, it was the unengaged life that was not worth living.

Do we call this naïve, quixotic, reckless, mad? Possibly. That is certainly what many people said about the quest of Barack Obama and his supporters for the U.S. presidency after eight dark years of George W. Bush, with his torture and lies and other abuses of power. "Yes, we can," was the mantra of change—and, yes, it did happen.

Perhaps such resistance stems from psychological flaws, such as an inability to imagine the might of the evil and the fragility of the resistance in comparison. On the other hand, it may be that the resisters' imagination is so strong because they can envision an end to the evil. Whatever the inner motivation, the power of resistance is real. Without those who stand up for justice, where would the rest of us be? Gisa, our heroine, is an example to emulate, and *Silence Not A Love Story* prods us to act upon the call to justice.

Elizabeth Holtzman, *the youngest woman elected to Congress, served for 8 years. She won national attention for her role during the Watergate hearings on impeachment of President Nixon. In Congress, she exposed the presence of Nazi war criminals in the U.S. and created the legal and administrative structure for bringing them to justice. She was later appointed by President Clinton to a panel responsible for declassifying the secret U.S. files on Nazi war criminals. Holtzman is also the first woman ever elected Brooklyn District Attorney and New York City Comptroller. As a Harvard law student, she worked in civil rights in the South. Currently, she practices law in New York City.*

SILENCE NOT A Love Story

Prologue: The World of the Play
by Cynthia L. Cooper

Silence Not A Love Story opens a window to a time and place in which the course of history was shifting. The rise of the Nazi movement in Germany in the late 1920s and early 1930s, permitting the ascension of Adolf Hitler to a position of power on January 30, 1933, led to consequences that the world came to know all too well.

This time period also marked the coming of age of Gisa Peiper, the young Jewish woman at the center of *Silence Not A Love Story*. An honors graduate of a German high school (gymnasium) with a passion for art, literature, and justice, she moved from her family's modest quarters in Berlin to Hamburg in 1929 at the age of nineteen. There, she joined with a small liberal political group involved in the labor movement and met Paul Konopka, a young Catholic craftsman. Soon, despite dangers and hardships, both became involved in anti-Nazi activities.

I first learned about Gisa Peiper's story from friends in Minnesota, where Gisa settled after World War II (see the *Postscript* to the play). Like many people, especially those of us who grew up in Jewish families, I struggled to understand what had happened in Germany. What, I wondered, would I have done in that place, at that time? How would I have reacted? What characteristics of mine would rise to the surface, and propel me forward?

Less is written about the time period of the late 1920s and early 1930s when the Nazis built their forces than about the years that follow. And what literature does exist about this time period is inevitably colored with the harsh memories of what happened later. But there are potent lessons of love and courage and resistance -- the world that I entered in *Silence Not A Love Story*.

In 1929, as the economy crashed in the United States, Germany reeled from a decade of economic, political, and social distress following World War I. The Weimar Republic, the new parliamentary democracy created in 1919 to replace the constitutional monarchy of the Kaiser, was untested, and, as it turned out, also unstable. The experiment ended fourteen years later when Hitler maneuvered his way into control of the reins of power.

While this time period roiled with severe political and economic challenges, Germany also crackled with innovation. Art, literature, music, and science thrived in the 1920s with Expressionist poets, Bauhaus architecture, modern art, cabaret clubs, cafes, street theatre, and, to the dismay of reactionary traditionalists like Hitler and his right-wing cohorts, the youthful casting-off of taboos. Young people explored philosophy, psychology, political engagement, and liberalized social mores. All of these nascent movements would be slammed to a halt once Hitler came into power.

The Weimar Republic itself faced innumerable difficulties from the outset. The conclusion of the First World War landed hard. Many Germans, especially former soldiers, believed that victory had been at hand, but that the nation had been betrayed by a conspiracy of internal and international forces. Jews were especially blamed. The Versailles Treaty of 1919, to which the new government had assented, was widely viewed as oppressive, humiliating, and unfair. Its excessive reparations and trade barriers placed Germany in an economic stranglehold. Unemployment was astronomical, inflation soared, and money was virtually worthless. The disbandment of the bulk of the military left World War I soldiers tetherless.

Political parties proliferated in that period, but no single party held a majority. On the right and the left, political factions and fractures stood in the way of effective governing. Even before the new democracy could take hold, Communists tried to stage a revolution in late 1918, which was quelled with brutal force and the aid of paramilitary forces, causing further fissures.

On the left, the largest political group, the Social Democratic Party or SPD, split, and two new parties formed -- the Independent Social Democratic Party of Germany (USPD) and the Majority Social Democrats, MSDP or SPD. In the election of the first national assembly of the Reichstag (parliament), several other parties gained votes, including the Catholic Centre party, the left-liberal German Democratic party, the national-liberal German People's Party, and the conservative and nationalist German National People's Party.

Into this mix entered the ultra-conservative German Workers' Party in Munich, or DAP. Adolf Hitler, an Austrian-born soldier who fought with the German Army in World War I, attended a meeting in 1919. By 1920, the group changed its name to the National Socialist German Workers' Party, known as the Nazis (from the contraction of "national" and "socialist"), and Hitler became its leader. Among its platforms were German nationalism, denunciation of the Versailles Treaty, single-party dictatorship, fierce anti-communism, a state-controlled economy, and repression of the Jews by laws and by force. Within two years, the Nazis added a paramilitary organization, the Storm Troopers, also known as the SA or simply the Brown Shirts. In addition to serving as bodyguards, its members were quick to engage in street fighting, terrorism, and assault, and were widely viewed as ruthless bullies.

Reactionary elements in Germany simmered elsewhere, as well. In 1922, young paramilitaries murdered the liberal foreign minister Walther Rathenau, a widely-admired Jewish and German patriot. Rathenau "belongs, without doubt, to the five or six great personalities of this century," wrote the German journalist Sebastian Haffner in a manuscript prepared before World War II but only published much later as the book *Defying Hitler*. "If my experience of Germany has taught me anything, it is this: Rathenau and Hitler are the two men who excited the imagination of the German masses to the utmost; the one by his ineffable culture, the other by his ineffable vileness."

Hitler displayed his methodology by rallying Nazi followers to stage a coup in Munich in 1923. The SA surrounded a beer hall where government officials were meeting, placed armed guards at the door, and marched into the building. Hitler leapt onto the stage with a pistol, yelling "Silence," and declared that the Bavarian government was being overthrown and replaced by the Nazis. The next day, the police fought the Nazis in the streets, and overcame them. Hitler was arrested, but managed to use his trial to get public attention for Nazi beliefs. Convicted, he was sent to prison, where he dictated his autobiography, "Mein Kampf." In it, he lays out his political philosophy, declaring the racial superiority of the "master race" of Nordic "Aryans," and insisting upon the inferiority of Slavs, Gypsies, and especially Jews, who were described as a menace that needed to be eliminated.

In 1924, after serving only nine months of a five-year sentence, Hitler was released from prison. Even though the Nazi party had been banned for a year, within two months, Hitler rebuilt it and began to aggressively chart a course to secure power through means that could be seen as legal. The Nazis began to run candidates in the national elections, building up support with fake promises of help for workers and families, and actively terrorizing opponents along the way.

Gisa Peiper and Paul Konopka, growing into political awareness in the late 1920s, were drawn to a very different type of politics. Gisa had grown up in Berlin, the middle of three sisters. Gisa's parents, Bronia and Mendel, were observant Jews who had each emigrated from Poland as youth. After they met in Berlin and married, Mendel opened a small bakery and grocery; its two rooms also served as the family's cramped living quarters. During World War I, Mendel fought for Germany, leaving Bronia to the challenging task of running the business alone with her daughters. When Mendel returned, the family, like others in Germany, faced economic uncertainty. Financially pressured, Gisa's father forbade her from attending high school, but Gisa, an ardent student, persisted in her determination to continue her education, and finally won his assent.

Paul, a few years senior to Gisa, grew up in Hamburg. His Catholic family had roots in Silesia, a border area that was at times part of Germany, at times part of Poland. Paul's father was largely absent from the home, and was violent and abusive when present. For survival, Paul's mother worked long hours in physically grueling factory jobs that eventually crippled her. Her circumstances were so dire during World War I that she sent Paul and his three siblings to live with relatives. When back at home, Paul helped support the family by becoming an apprentice to a builder of wood auto bodies. He continued his education informally by attending a special academy run by a small independent political party, the International Socialist Combat League, or the ISK.

The ISK philosophy also attracted Gisa Peiper, and it was through the ISK that she met Paul. Despite the "combat" in its name, the ISK was made up of pacifists and humanitarians. Politically, the group, was strongly opposed to Communism, but deeply connected to the labor movement. Its utopian views were developed by Leonard Nelson, a philosopher and professor. At its heart, the ISK insisted that people seek the truth and then act upon it. Nelson engaged in rigorous reasoning and critical thinking that sought to apply three basic questions—*What can we know? What should we do? What may we hope?* Members of the ISK studied political issues through group analyses and Socratic questioning, and they believed that action must follow understanding. With chapters in several cities, the ISK offered improvement programs, ran a school for young students (the one Paul attended), followed a vegetarian diet, and, most unusually for the times, shunned alcohol. Members of the ISK were energetic youth of varied economic and religious backgrounds who immersed themselves in politics and direct action, studying, working, volunteering, and spending leisure time together in hiking, swimming, and camping. After Leonard Nelson died unexpectedly in 1927, the ISK continued under the leadership of Willie Eichler and Minna Specht, among others.

The ISK stood 180 degrees apart from the Nazis, which prescribed a reactionary policy and demanded absolute fealty. In and out of power, the Nazis used violence, intimidation, and terror against those who opposed them. Paul and Gisa were among those who saw the Nazis as a dangerous development and a growing threat. Their anti-Nazi resistance efforts were a natural extension of that understanding.

Later Gisa recalled: "Most everybody knew what the Nazis stood for before the Nazis came to power. Their terror tactics showed in street fights, in writings, in threats before they came to final power. The demeaning and torturing of anyone resisting them started immediately after January 1933. Fear pervaded the country. Everybody (I exclude the children) knew about the terror. It was also known outside of Germany. Yet people did not *want* to believe those atrocities, or hoped to be on the side of the Nazis, whom they perceived as invincible."

The Nazis mounted an ugly and fierce opposition to the liberal democracy with the goal of ending the Weimar Republic. Supported by industrialists who saw them as the next best thing to restoration of the monarchy and the privileges they enjoyed under it, the Nazis relentlessly campaigned against Jews, Communists, and those who they claimed had "stabbed Germany in the back." The Nazis never secured a majority in open elections. In April 1932, President Paul von Hindenburg defeated Hitler, who had just become a German citizen, in a runoff for the presidency. The Nazi party received its highest number of votes in July 1932, winning 37.3 percent of the seats in the Reichstag. In November 1933, the last free election, the numbers dropped, and the Nazis received only 33.1 percent of the vote.

Still, some powerful people believed that they needed to reckon with the Nazis and their paramilitary street forces. The elderly president von Hindenburg was convinced by others that Hitler could be better managed from the inside. With the government unable to stabilize and Nazis blocking progress, the president offered the position of Chancellor (the other major leadership office in the German system) to Hitler on January 30, 1933. The ground began to shift in Germany almost immediately.

Hitler moved to secure absolute control. Within days, all political demonstrations were banned. Within a month, the Reichstag was set on fire, and although Communists were blamed, the Nazis undoubtedly were responsible. Hitler then secured emergency powers of control, and Communist members of the Reichstag were arrested. Within two months, the SA, still active, unleashed riots and attacks against Jews. The Reichstag gave Hitler dictatorial powers, and closed down. At a rapid pace, Hitler moved against dissidents, opponents, and Jews, with decrees, propaganda, intimidation, boycotts, physical violence, detention, and arrests. In short, the Third Reich took hold.

Gisa later wrote: "There was resistance against the Nazis inside Germany consisting of a variety of people who had a conscience and courage. These people included Jews (who are unjustly accused of never having resisted), women (who are practically omitted in the history of resistance), and non-Jewish Germans, as well as many of the old labor movements (who are hardly mentioned). They fought the Nazis out of basically moral convictions and out of abhorrence of racial superiority."

This is the world of *Silence Not A Love Story*. The story is about one period in history, but it may inform other periods, and shed light on our own courage or strength in the face of forces that seem damaging, destructive, or inhumane.

I felt drawn to Gisa's story because I wanted to know more about the fiber and mettle of people who stand up to oppression — in that time, and in our time. When world situations rub against the values of human rights that I hold dear, and people are treated with indifference or callousness or disregard for all that is just and fair, what are we — what am I — called to do? I don't have exact answers, but now I have a better grasp of the questions: *What can we know? What should we do? What may we hope?*

If I could inscribe four sentences on my play, they would be these words from Gisa: "I want to convey a basic conviction about human beings. They carry in them the seeds of destruction as well as great love and giving. It will depend on us, each person within each generation at all times, what we help to bring forth. This is an unending task."

—Cynthia L. Cooper

Characters, Time & Place

Characters:

GISA PEIPER—Born in 1910, GISA, a young Jewish woman, moves from Berlin to Hamburg in 1929 at age 19 to participate with that city's chapter of the International Socialist Kombat League (ISK), a labor and political organization founded by pacifist Leonard Nelson. The young idealists who participate in the ISK seek to build a more equitable society in this time of combustible economic and political circumstances. GISA, an avid learner with deep passions for art, poetry and justice, comes from modest circumstances. Her parents, MENDEL and BRONIA, operate a bakery and store in Berlin, but are not happy with their daughter's freethinking path and youthful political exuberance. GISA ranges from 19-28 in the play.

ADRIANA KUEHN—Seen throughout the entire play, ADRIANA is the same person as GISA, above. She is 28 years old and using false papers as she sits in the Munich train station for two hours awaiting a transfer to Paris. All of her dialogue is her inner thinking. Other than two words, she never speaks in real-time. Although only 28, she has aged greatly in nine years.

PAUL KONOPKA—A labor and resistance activist and member of the ISK, PAUL grew up in Hamburg. He is 23 in 1929 when he meets GISA Peiper and they become companions. PAUL comes from a working class Catholic family living in harsh circumstances. A craftsman who works with his hands, he has clear and direct political instincts and a penchant for argument.

HILDE HOCH—A member of the ISK in Hamburg, she grew up as close friends with PAUL and becomes a confidante of GISA. She is 22 in 1929.

FRANZ HABERMAN—A printer's apprentice, FRANZ is a Jewish man in Hamburg who works with the ISK as a labor activist and resistance worker. He is approximately 24 in 1929.

WILLIE EICHLER—Leader, along with Minna Specht, of the International Socialist Kombat League, a labor and political organization founded by pacifist Leonard Nelson.

FRIEDA—GISA's landlady in Hamburg, she is 30 years old and a mother of one in 1929.

THE WOMAN in MUNICH STATION—Weaving throughout the station while ADRIANA waits for a train on the day of Austria's capitulation to German rule, or Anschluss, she entertains soldiers and keeps a present and watchful eye on ADRIANA. SHE ultimately has a critical role in the play.

SOLDIER 1 at MUNICH STATION—A Nazi Reich soldier who is thrilled with Anschluss.

SOLDIER 2 at MUNICH STATION—A few years older than SOLDIER 1 but of similar ideas.

MENDEL PEIPER—A deeply religious Jewish man, MENDEL is GISA's father. He owns a small bakery in Berlin, living in the room next door. After fleeing from Poland as a child, he is married to BRONIA and has two other daughters: Ruth (younger than GISA) and Hanna (older than GISA). After fighting in World War I for Germany, he is embittered and cynical.

BRONIA PEIPER—GISA's mother, she works alongside her husband, MENDEL.

PROF. KALTENBACH—A professor at Hamburg University.

GESTAPO MAN—A person assigned to question prisoners.

OLD MAN GUARD—A longtime worker at the Fuhlsbüttel prison.

UNDERGROUND WORKER—A person who assists people fleeing Germany.

Minor Characters (appearing and explained in text):

PASSERSBY
FACTORY WORKER
OFF-STAGE TRAIN STATION ANNOUNCER
MADDALEN
MADDALEN's BOYFRIEND
POLICE OFFICER
WOMAN ON HAMBURG STREETS
NEWSBOY
TWO SS HAMBURG
TWO SS MUNICH
TWO GUARDS
WOMAN PRISON TRUSTEE
CZECH DOCTOR
AUSTRIAN MAN (MR. KUEHN)

Cast breakdown for 7 actors: *Silence Not A Love Story* may be performed by seven actors: four women and three men.

1 (W)—GISA, age 19-28

2 (W)—ADRIANA, age 28 (but looking older)

3 (W)—HILDE (age 22-29) (multiple scenes), FACTORY WORKER (I-6), HAMBURG WOMAN (II-9), NEWSBOY (II-15), GUARD (II-18), UNDERGROUND WORKER (II-23)

4 (W)—FRIEDA (age 30-37) (multiple scenes), WOMAN IN MUNICH STATION (multiple scenes), BENCH PERSON (I-3), MADDALEN (I-9), BRONIA (II-4, II-23), MUNICH SS II (II-17), GUARD (II-18), PRISON TRUSTEE (II-20)

5 (M)—PAUL (age 23-30) (multiple scenes), SS I HAMBURG (II-17), GESTAPO (II-18), CZECH DOCTOR (II-23)

6 (M)—FRANZ (age 24-31) (multiple scenes), SOLDIER 2 (multiple scenes), MADDALEN BOYFRIEND (I-9), SS II HAMBURG (II-17), SS GUARD (II-21)

7 (M)—MENDEL (age 55) (I-17, II-4), SOLDIER 1 (multiple scenes), WILLIE EICHLER (I-4, I-11) O.S. ANNOUNCER (I-8, II-21), PROF. KALTENBACH (II-7), POLICE OFFICER (II-9), MUNICH SS I (II-17), OLD MAN GUARD (II-19), MR. KUEHN (II-23)

TIME AND PLACE

The time of the play is the exciting — but volatile — political and economic landscape of Germany from 1929 to 1938 when a new generation is discovering the realities of a harsh future, and idealists mount resistance to a growing right wing.

The play opens in a train station in Munich in March, 1938. The Munich train station is a constant and continuous presence throughout the entirety of the play. Other scenes in the play take place in Hamburg, Berlin, and also, briefly, in Czechoslovakia. The author anticipates a set that is evocative as much as realistic.

AUTHOR'S NOTES

All of the characters in this play are German, although of varying backgrounds. In real life, the characters would speak fluent German. In the text of the play, all of the language is in English.

This play is based on real incidents and drawn, in part, from stories and experiences described in "Courage and Love," a memoir by Dr. Gisa Konopka, and used with permission. Poetry used in the play by others than the author or Gisa Peiper Konopka is by Charles Theodore Henri de Coster ("Life I wrote on my banner"); Georg Heym ("White clouds grow"); Henrik Ibsen ("Her home lies on a sea of freedom"); Else Lasker-Schuler ("I have a blue piano"); Ruth Peiper ("And by a lonely fireside" "They have made us into aged beings" "And when they grinned and spat"); Ranier Maria Rilke ("When dogs are sleeping"); Avestan Zarathushtra ("When will it start").

SILENCE NOT
A LOVE STORY

ACT ONE

Scene 1: Munich Train Station, March 1938.

The interior of a train station in Munich, March 1938. The blowing of the wind turns into the blow of a whistle. People rush to the window. A flurry of activity occurs when the train stops. German soldiers rush in, a band begins to play lively cabaret music. Women and men begin to hug and twirl one another about as if it were a dance. There is a great rush and ebullience and full-fisted joy. Several German soldiers celebrate with THE WOMAN, who greets them joyfully, passing out steins of beer.

> SOLDIER 1: To Austria!

> THE WOMAN: From all of us in Munich! Austrians... we welcome you to the Fatherland!

ADRIANA enters, looks around, takes a seat on a bench, as if trying to be invisible. THE SOLDIERS pay no attention to her, but carry on with their celebration. THE WOMAN watches ADRIANA closely. She takes stock of ADRIANA, walks up to her and broadly holds out a stein.

> THE WOMAN: A toast on me! Drink up! A two-hour layover between Vienna and Paris is no good on your own. Celebrate! To Anschluss!

ADRIANA waves 'no' and moves down on the bench. THE WOMAN continues to observe her.

> SOLIDER 2: To Anschluss! The Union!

> SOLDIER 1: Austria: ours without a single shot! Remember this date: March 12, 1938! Austria and Germany in union!

ADRIANA looks around, as if to note the date.

> SOLDIERS & THE WOMAN: To the Third Reich!

Silence Not A Love Story   15

SOLDIERS: To a thousand years!

ADRIANA *nods and smiles slightly. She tries to look much older than she is. She pulls a scarf around her head, and coughs as if she is sick, although she is not. A SOLDIER offers her a stein again, she coughs and waves it off. SHE sits. She sits. SHE sits.*

A woman dressed identically—GISA—*comes up and stands behind* ADRIANA. *They are the same person, but GISA is an inner vision, a person in a different time, a different place, nine years earlier. GISA puts her hands on* ADRIANA's *shoulders.*

ADRIANA's *text is inner monologue. Except for two words in the play, she never speaks in a normal realistic conversation. The words of her text feel intimate to the audience, her thoughts climbing inside their heads, as if coming through headphones and projecting mind to mind.* ADRIANA *never leaves the Munich Station, and the station is a presence throughout the play. Her voice is mesmerizingly real.*

    ADRIANA & GISA: *(Simultaneous.)*
Don't!
Hold steady!
Remember the name on the visa.
Don't say a word!

    ADRIANA: *(Speaking alone.)*
Don't laugh.
Don't cry.
Don't smile.
Don't sing.

Don't.

Don't joke.
Don't wink.
Don't wince.
Don't blink.

16 Silence Not A Love Story

Don't.

Don't, Gisa.

GISA swings around and shakes ADRIANA momentarily.

GISA: No.

ADRIANA: No. No... that's not your name! Your new name. Think only of your new name. The name on your visa. The Austrian name they've given you. Adriana. Yes. Adriana. Think 'Adriana.' Don't, Adriana. Don't forget. Don't forget. Don't forget.

Scene Two: Hamburg Train Station, October 1929.

GISA peels away from ADRIANA and rushes into a different light. It's nine years earlier in 1929 at a different train station, this one in Hamburg, Germany. GISA is carting a small suitcase and another bag, large enough to hold art prints. HILDE, a young German woman, stands nearby, holding a scrap of paper.

ADRIANA stays seated on the train bench in Munich throughout the scene. ADRIANA watches. Occasionally ADRIANA moves slightly, to take out a handkerchief or to eat a nut, carefully pulled out of her pocket, as we enter the world of GISA.

GISA approaches HILDE tentatively.

GISA: A clock? Do you know where I can find one?

HILDE: *SHE points to a clock above.* 12:50 already. I've been waiting nearly two hours for the train from Berlin. Still no sign. *She shows a piece of paper.* See: October 29, 1929, arriving 11:02, Berlin to Hamburg.

ADRIANA: *Speaking across time and space to GISA.*
1929? Barely nine years ago?

GISA: *Speaks to ADRIANA.*
Yes, yes.
Now shhh.
They must not hear your accent.
Say nothing.

ADRIANA:
Nothing at all.
I'm swimming.
Diving down to touch the rocks.

GISA:
Dive deep.

GISA: *Turns to HILDE.* I was on the 11:02. We stalled. A man in my compartment opened the window and looked up and down. "They're working. Sixty kilometers down the track," he said. Then he closed the window, put on his hat, and in five minutes, repeated the whole thing, as if it were an art performance. "They're working. Sixty kilometers down the track."

I was to meet someone near the clock. From a club. A political club.

HILDE: *Now interested.* You look entirely too young for a political club.

GISA: I'm not. I finished my high school examinations last week.

HILDE: *Begins to look around again.* The person I'm waiting for wouldn't have a degree, not like that. We're working people.

GISA: I'm a working person. I deliver the morning bread rolls for my father's bakery.

HILDE: *Suddenly, with renewed interest.* Did you eat one on the journey?

GISA: Only half. If you're hungry...?
Looking in her bag, SHE sees something, pulls out gloves.
Oh! I forgot! My gloves!

HILDE: Is it a sausage roll?

GISA: No. I'm a vegetarian. It's part of my...

HILDE: But you washed in down with a hearty ale...?

GISA: "Drinking workers don't think and thinking workers don't drink." Part of my membership...

HILDE:... in the ISK! Then you're Gisa Peiper?

GISA: Yes! That's what I'm trying to say.

HILDE: You're supposed to be wearing white gloves.

GISA: It's not cold. I couldn't pretend.

HILDE: This is how I'm to recognize you. Security measures! My leg is still purple from the labor rally last week—smashed. Didn't they warn you about that right-winger and his goons in brown shirts?

GISA: "In Munich," they said.

HILDE: His "biography" is at every bookstall. "'My Struggle' by Adolph Hitler." Imagine this: A man came to our ISK offices in Hamburg, thinking that we—the International Socialist Kombat League—is somehow connected to the National Socialists!

GISA: As if the ISK and the Nazis...

HILDE:... have anything in common!

GISA: Not to know the left from the right!

HILDE: Exactly my point. The instructions said: "She will wear white gloves, stand by the clock and say the words 'bread roll.'"

GISA: I'll do better in the future. I promise.

HILDE: Very well.

Hello! I'm Hilde Hoch, the official greeting committee for the Hamburg International Socialist Kombat League! We in the ISK are pleased to welcome a new member moving all the way from Berlin! And now, hurry, please.

As this scene occurs, ADRIANA, sitting in the Munich station, is approached by SOLDIER 2, who offers a cigarette.

SOLDIER: Smoke?
GISA calls across time and space to ADRIANA.

GISA: Careful! CAREful. Don't forget.

ADRIANA waves 'no' to the soldier, coughs, points to her throat, coughs again.
The SOLDIER moves on.

ADRIANA:
I can't breathe.
I'll drown.
Why Munich?

GISA: *Speaks to ADRIANA.*
Sit. Stay. Swim.
It's only two hours.
Follow the instructions.
Sit, wait, say nothing.

ADRIANA:
Words are choking in my throat.
My heartbeat is racing.
My eyes...

GISA:
Don't cry.

No emotion.
Pretend.
Float! You can float!

>ADRIANA:
>Yes, yes.
>You're right.
>Yes.

GISA: *Turns back to HILDE.* What if we hadn't found each other? I can hear my father. "What kind of foolish daughter did I raise to put her faith in some left-wing political group!"

HILDE: "Hard work and prayer."

GISA: Yes, that's him.

HILDE: Then, parents in Berlin and Hamburg are all the same!

GISA: Does your father also quote Abraham, Moses and the Rebbe?

HILDE: My father has pious Lutherans. "Young lady, I expect you to be a model for the younger children... so you must not sleep during the sermon!"

GISA: *SHE laughs with HILDE.* They should be reading Freud instead. Or Adler.

HILDE: Only the young people have a clue! Only freethinkers like us! *HILDE pulls out literature. SHE speaks confidentially.* The Hamburg ISK is my family! We have discussions on Monday, committees on Wednesday, tutors on Friday. Workdays on Saturday. And on Sundays, we go... to church!

GISA: *(Alarmed.)* To church? But...

HILDE: I'm teasing! On Sundays, we go for a hike! As set out by Leonard Nelson himself. And Minna Specht and Willie Eichler. Sunday is reserved for a long, glorious hike up the Elbe. Or a swim.

>ADRIANA:
>Float.

I want to float.

GISA: But... does the ISK know of any jobs?

HILDE: In the morning, I'll show you the bottle factory. But say goodbye to your pretty hands.

GISA: A factory is perfect. I can learn more about labor rights from the inside out.

HILDE: Very well. But at the moment, we're late. *(SHE reaches for GISA's folder.)*

GISA: Oh, no. I'll carry that. They're prints, art prints; special. From a friend. Rudy. In Berlin.

HILDE: *SHE takes a different bag.*

So Gisa Peiper has her degree AND a 'friend' in Berlin.

GISA: Oh no. Rudy's a... platonic friend. He's different. We go to museums. We love art together. But life would be so lonely without friends, don't you agree?

Scene 3: Munich Train Station, 1938.

A PERSON sits near ADRIANA; SHE adjusts slightly, holds up a handkerchief and coughs. The PERSON on the bench moves away. SOLDIER 1 crosses and nods to the PERSON on the bench, who holds out her hand in a warm hello.

ADRIANA:
Remember. Remember.
There is always some good.
Remember Gisa.
Remember Adriana.
Remember.
Remember, remember.

Don't dwell.
Don't frown.
Don't scowl.
Don't pout.
Don't dwell.
Don't dwell.
Don't dwell.
Remember the good.

There is always
Some
Good.

Scene 4: Hamburg, ISK Headquarters, 1929.

HILDE and GISA join a small group in the basement office of the ISK near the Reeperbahn, a bawdy district.

PAUL is leaning over a table, working. HE is pleasant but has a dark air. He's stocky and not a pretty boy; strong, but not athletic. Although young, his face shows the hard edges of life. HILDE addresses everyone.

HILDE: Two new hands to help! Everyone, say hello to our new member!

PAUL does not look up and, almost imperceptibly, turns his back, as HILDE watches.

GISA: Hello.

HILDE: We're making a banner: "FAIR WAGES."

HILDE sits GISA at the table, then taps PAUL and pulls him aside to talk privately.

HILDE: Paul— may I have a moment, please?

GISA studies the banner. PAUL swirls away from HILDE and walks over to GISA. HE holds out his hand, palm up.

GISA: A needle? Thank you. I can join right in on the banner.

PAUL joins in cutting, measuring, sewing the banner.

PAUL: Hilde tells me I must speak to you.

GISA: And do you always do what Hilde tells you?

PAUL: I never do what Hilde tells me. That's why I offered the needle. You spoke to me. I didn't speak.

GISA: But what if I were not the type who is nimble with a needle?

PAUL: Then you would learn. Hilde says you came to Hamburg to study 'labor.' Although we generally labor just fine without some Berlin girl coming to poke and probe.

GISA: I see. Let me ask, how can children get an education if they can't eat a decent meal? And how can they eat a decent meal if their parents can't earn a decent wage? I've seen children on the street so hungry that they don't even have the energy for stickball. The ISK said this was the place to study the trade union movement.

PAUL: Those are your reasons?

GISA: I see now that it may have been a mistake.

FRANZ, another member of the ISK, bursts in, carrying a machine aloft, excited.

FRANZ: Look! A Gestetner! For printing! My boss was throwing it out because it leaves little blobs on the paper! But it still works!

HILDE hugs FRANZ warmly.

HILDE: Our own machine! Franz—it's a dream come true!

FRANZ: We can print flyers, notices. A newsletter! Let's dance! Dance the Gestetner with me!

In a surprising move, PAUL does a sudden dance step.

PAUL: I'm ready. I have a stack of write-ups!

HILDE: And I'll bet our new member can write a sentence from beginning to end without losing the thought. Gisa—has a degree!

Hilde points to GISA. FRANZ goes and gives her a hearty handshake.

FRANZ: Hello Gisa!

GISA: Only a high school degree.

HILDE: What did I say! She can write!

GISA: Mostly poetry. In my journal. Privately.

FRANZ: It's settled! Gisa will be the editor of our new newsletter! Which will have poetry AND stories. And we will print it on the Gestetner!

HILDE: A spark of genius. Ohh! "The Spark!" For the masthead! You'll do it, won't you, Gisa?

GISA: "The Spark" sounds like a fine name. *(SHE pauses)* Very well. I... accept.

FRANZ: It's agreed. First edition, next month: "The Spark. Dateline, November 1929 Hamburg ISK." *FRANZ and HILDE toy with each other and the machine.*

PAUL: *(To GISA)* Now that you are the Editor in charge of verses and paragraphs, I suppose you no longer wish to sew a mere letter.

GISA: (Laughs.) Tell me, is it because I'm from Berlin, or want better conditions for workers, or am female, that upsets you most? Or are you this contemptuous of everyone you meet?

PAUL: What kind of question is that?

GISA: I'm wondering what you are good at. Other than starting arguments.

PAUL: I AM very good at arguing.

GISA: I understand that—sir.

PAUL: Konopka. Gerhardt. You may call me Paul.

GISA: And, tell me, Paul, what else do you do?

PAUL: I can make almost anything that can be made with the hands.

Banner, woodcut, painting. If I weren't a poor boy from Hamburg with a gloomy view of the world, I might be a famous artist.

GISA: An artist can have a gloomy view.

PAUL: Only an artist who doesn't do art.

GISA: And what about Käthe Kollwitz?

PAUL: Ahh. Käthe Kollwitz. She doesn't have a gloomy view. She's an idealist who shows gloom to the world in order to effect change.

GISA: Then what of her poster for the German Home Workers Exhibition of 1906?

PAUL: This is a drawing of an ordinary woman laborer, undeniably trapped in miserable circumstances, and utterly aware of her situation. Kollwitz illuminates her humanity.

GISA: *(After pausing a moment.)* I met her.

PAUL: Who?

GISA: Käthe Kollwitz. At a protest against fascism in Italy. I was handing out leaflets. And there she was in the crowd. So I went up to her and spoke.

PAUL: You're a bold one.

GISA: First, I put the literature in her hand. *(She demonstrates)* And then I burst out, "Excuse me, Miss Kollwitz—I must tell you how much your art means to me."

PAUL: And?

GISA: She turned her head up from the leaflet and looked at me from under her eyelids, heavy and wide. Like this. *(GISA imitates.)* Then she said: "You are young and full of ideals. Promise me you will remember this also when you are old."

PAUL: That's good. "Remember this also when you are old."

      ADRIANA: Promise me.

GISA: *SHE talks to ADRIANA now.* 'When you are old.'

ADRIANA: I'm not old.

GISA: Promise me.

ADRIANA: 28 is NOT old.

GISA: Promise me to GET old.

ADRIANA:
They left a knife on the table.
Spare us the trouble,
they said.
You can end your pathetic woes.
We've left something for you.
On the table.

And now.
This.
You must wait for the layover.
Only two hours.

Two hours is too long.

GISA: Promise.

GISA: *SHE talks to PAUL, now.* And I said: "I promise, Miss Kollwitz. I WILL remember." And then my friend Rudy gave me her prints for my graduation. There—

GISA points to the folder carried from the train station. PAUL steps in that direction as if he's going to open the folder.

PAUL: Let's see

GISA: *GISA suddenly blocks his path.*

I'm afraid I don't know you well enough, Mr. Konopka.

Silence Not A Love Story 27

PAUL: My manners are bad.

GISA: No...

PAUL: *PAUL suddenly changes course.* No matter. I'm not afraid to show you my art, Miss Peiper. *HE takes a pin and twists it.* One piece only. The rest of my artwork is reserved for my tutor.

GISA: And who is your tutor?

PAUL: My tutor teaches me advanced German, composition and poetry. I'll add manners. Except—I only have an application for a tutor, not a real live tutor.

GISA: No doubt, your turn will come. You mustn't have a gloomy view.

PAUL: The young woman from Berlin twists my words. *(Opens his hand to a figurine twisted with the pin.)* For you, a private viewing of the latest work from that Hamburg artist, Gerhardt Paul Konopka!

HILDE: *SHE breaks away from FRANZ.* Hello! Willie Eichler is coming. Look busy.

HILDE and FRANZ start working on the banner.

PAUL: Miss Peiper and I have been busy!

HILDE: Shh.

WILLIE enters. HE is the national leader of the ISK, which is an acronym for the International Socialist Combat (or Kombat) League, one of many small political groups in Germany at the time. The group was founded by Leonard Nelson, a "freethinker" and former professor. Nelson himself died at a young age in the mid 1920s, but the group carries on based on his writings and a school that he founded. The ISK draws people from varied religious and class backgrounds and follows a humanistic whole-life philosophy. Serious study is combined with activism; work and volunteer activities are mingled with hikes and exercise. The group is pro-labor, but anti-Communist; members are pacifists, vegetarians and nondrinkers. In a fashion later observed in 1960s and '70s American activism, ISK members engage in Socratic dialogue and consciousness-raising, analyzing problems from personal, political and theoretical perspectives, combining history, art, philosophy, and, most radical for the time, psychology. Members not only study and work together, they socialize and sometimes live together, as well.

WILLIE: Everyone's so busy! Good, good.

HILDE: Stitching a new banner.

WILLIE: I'm visiting every chapter. *(HE pulls out a newspaper.)* Look. "STOCK MARKET CRASH IN AMERICA SETS OFF NEW WORLD FEARS."

HILDE: More trouble headed our way!

FRANZ: And it's always the workers who get it in the teeth.

PAUL: You can count on us to get out there right away with the truth. Even if I have to stay here all night. "NO LAYOFFS. NO CUTBACKS. WORKERS HAVE RIGHTS."

WILLIE: I knew I could depend on the chapter in Hamburg.

WILLIE nods in gratitude, exits. PAUL steps up the work pace.

GISA: You're true to your word, Mr. Konopka: your hands have many talents.

PAUL: Even a poor boy from Hamburg can have assets. There is good everywhere.

PAUL twirls away. GISA picks up her packages and leaves.

>ADRIANA: *(Sitting in the Munich Station.)*
>And by a lonely fireside let gleam
>your fairy castle built of ruby and of jade
>and it will never die and never fade.
>
>There is always
>Some
>Good.

Scene 5: Hamburg, An Apartment, 1929.

FRIEDA, a Hamburg woman, leads GISA through a mid-sized apartment, arriving at a single room.

FRIEDA: I have no choice but to rent out my second room. Everyone's money is tight. *(Points.)* Here it is.

GISA: My own room! I can build a library.

FRIEDA: I don't want to know. You pay your rent. You don't put any holes in the walls with plaques and pictures and the like. You mind your business.

GISA: Of course.

FRIEDA: By that, I mean, you mind yours, I mind mine.

GISA: Yes.

> ADRIANA: *From the Munich Station, where she sits.* It's the same year?
>
> GISA: *To ADRIANA.* Of course.
>
> ADRIANA:
> It seems so much longer ago.
>
> They have made us into aged beings,
> We, who dreamed,
> and hunted simple truths,
> we, who thirsted,
> and sought droplets of justice,
> now touch in our hair the light grey
> of an autumn day
> that begins with the mist
> and ends with the rain.
> Everything's changed.

GISA: *To ADRIANA.* Please; hush.

FRIEDA: I'll tell you right off. I have a daughter, ten years old. Lilla. Born on the same exact day as the Versailles Treaty... she was the only light in that horrid end to that horrid War. Her father was killed before he saw her. My brother, too. You lose anyone?

GISA: My father fought. *SHE pauses.* Then he returned. I used to take bread to the wounded.

FRIEDA: Then you don't know what it's like. This used to be my daughter's room. With the way things are, I'm forced to make concessions. She sleeps in my room.

GISA: I see.

FRIEDA: Do you have a boyfriend?

GISA: Oh no, nothing like that. I only recently moved here from Berlin and...

FRIEDA: You're one of those "very serious" young girls that my cousin Hilde knows.

GISA: I have employment: the bottle factory. And I enjoy things. Books. Art. Hikes! Swimming. I love to swim.

FRIEDA: I have a boyfriend. He comes around on Tuesday and Thursday. Saturday nights we go dancing, and come back here. Sunday he spends the day.

GISA: Very well.

FRIEDA: We're right in the next room. It's only a tiny apartment. Do you understand?

GISA: I think so.

FRIEDA: I need the rent.

GISA: I can pay one week in advance.

FRIEDA: I don't have anywhere for my daughter to be when Hans comes over.

GISA: I see.

FRIEDA: So?

GISA: She can come to my room. She can sleep on a pillow on the floor.

ADRIANA: *To GISA, across time.* You do this for her. But what about the men with boots? "Empty silence of endless soldiers' steps..." —Kandinsky. Remember?

GISA: *To ADRIANA.* Stop. You're confusing me.

ADRIANA: Yes. And when they come banging on the door? Late at night. With spit in their craw.

GISA: She's easily frightened.

ADRIANA: She's out for...

GISA: I'm ignoring you.

FRIEDA: We have an understanding, then.

GISA: Good. *SHE pulls out an envelope with money.*

FRIEDA: Mind you, I don't want you handing my daughter a lot of nonsense. Hilde's mixed up with some crazy political group. Whatever it is, I don't want to know. I need to rent the room. I want to listen to music at the beer hall on Saturday nights. Am I clear?

GISA: Very clear.

    ADRIANA:
Far away the twilight of something new,

moves slowly at first... miraculous.
Spirit alone cannot be action.

Action needs body and hand.
A form, a place, a motion.
There is song.
There is poetry.
There is art.
There is hope.

Scene 6: Hamburg, A Factory, 1930.

At the bottle factory, GISA sits with another woman, FACTORY WORKER, as they twist wire caps onto bottles. GISA speaks quietly.

GISA: I went to the union hall last night, spoke to the rep.

FACTORY WORKER: Yes? Can he help keep the same wages for each bottle cap?

GISA: He said they're blaming the crash. But it's only an excuse to squeeze us and cut the pay-per-cap. He said we should be getting a penny more for each bottle cap. He gave me a petition to pass.

FACTORY WORKER: I didn't bring my glasses.

GISA: It says that we are mothers and daughters who work long hours without breaks or adequate sanitary facilities, and that we are still not making enough to meet our daily needs.

FACTORY WORKER: It's true.

GISA: It says we're not seeking handouts, but we need a fair wage for our labor.

FACTORY WORKER: I'll sign.

SHE signs the petition. Soon, a whistle blows loudly. GISA and FACTORY WORKER, startled, stand abruptly.

Scene 7: Hamburg, Gisa's Room, 1930.

PAUL strides into GISA's room and sits. Books and little sculptures dot the room, and HE looks at them. GISA enters soon after.

PAUL: Tell the truth: there's no hope for an illiterate like me.

GISA: You do very well. A little advanced language, and you'll be scribbling like a famous philosopher, like Kant....

PAUL: So you agree there's no hope.

GISA: There's always hope.

PAUL: Then you agree that I'm an illiterate?

GISA: I agree that you're a contrarian, but you're not illiterate. It's an excuse for not doing your assignment. What did you bring?

PAUL: A pear. *HE pulls one out, cuts it, gives half to her.* How can I engage in advanced study when my tutor looks like she hasn't eaten in days?

GISA: You need glasses. Your eyes are playing tricks on you.

PAUL: Are you sending your bottle-factory earnings to some 'fellow'? Some 'Rudy'?

GISA: Rudy's a friend, not my 'fellow.' And, you're changing the topic.

PAUL: This is the problem. I'm burning to get certain facts in a certain order. Critical information from Munich. But my writing of it did not go well. I'm afraid my writing didn't get written.

GISA: Then it's impossible to help you improve it. We'll review grammar instead.

PAUL: I think something happened at your job that you're not telling me.

GISA: We can look at the conjugation of the verb. And then reflexive, impersonal, separable, inseparable and variable verbs.

PAUL: I did BRING something written. *HE stands, dramatically and grandiosely.*

"*Life I Wrote on My Banner.*"

Life I wrote on my banner
To live in the light
My first skin is made out of leather
But my second is made out of steel.

GISA: *Simultaneously.* "... my second is made out of steel." Folk poem: Till Eulenspiegel.

PAUL: Yes.

GISA: You read remarkably well.

PAUL: I memorized it.

GISA: Then you memorize remarkably well.

PAUL: My first skin is made of leather. You can talk to me and it won't hurt.

GISA: Tell me what you're burning to write.

PAUL: You tell me what's happened first.

GISA: You're impossible. Here it is: you were right to make fun of me. I was a fool to think that I could get a factory job and organize workers.

> ADRIANA:
> So many scars now.
> Don't touch the scars.
> Stay away from the scars.

PAUL: They let you go?

GISA: Me. Women with children. Women with elderly parents. We spend our days together at the unemployment office.

PAUL: Let me guess... you asked for an air vent.

GISA: They announced that the pay-per-piece was reduced. I brought a petition and all around our table, the women signed. Some with an X because that's all they can write. But when the closing bell came...

PAUL:... you were ordered to stand and march out.

GISA: In front of the whole factory. Out in the cold. Our whole table. I can't even bring myself to look them in the eye at unemployment.

PAUL: Why not! You helped them stand up for themselves, probably for the first time in their lives. That's an act of courage. I'm proud to have you as my tutor.

GISA: They trusted me, and I failed them.

PAUL: You don't get to take the blame! What choice did you have? Justice demands action.

Leaning forward. Honestly, I didn't come for tutoring. I need your help with an article for "The Spark."

GISA: The stories for this edition are all done.

PAUL: This is a matter of urgency. I went to Munich, undercover.

Scene 8: Munich Train Station, 1938.

> ADRIANA: What can be so urgent?
>
> ANNOUNCER *(INTERCOM)*: On Track 7, leaving Munich station in 10 minutes, Departure to points north: Nuremberg, Dresden, Dessau.
>
> ADRIANA: *SHE shakes her head.*
> I'm alone and you are far away
> Yet I feel your nearness so strongly,
> it is as if you stood closely to me
> And the wind's breath caressed us softly.
>
> It's urgent to say nothing.

The urgency is in the wait.
It cannot be helped if the wait is in Munich.
The waiting is the urgency.

Scene 9: Hamburg, Gisa's Room, 1930.

In a continuation of their conversation, PAUL and GISA sit in Gisa's quarters.

PAUL: The National Socialists are creating a private militia.

GISA: The Brown Shirts? They're not news. Every person in the Metalworkers union knows someone who's been roughed up.

PAUL: This is new. "Schutzstaffel" - that's what it's called. "SS" for short. They're conducting militia exercises in secret. Studying torture. A man named Himmler is the head. Heinrich Himmler.

GISA: They have no power. The whole "big" Nazi party barely holds a handful of seats in the Reichstag.

PAUL: In 1928, they had no parliamentary seats. Now, two years later, they've a handful of seats. And when the September election comes, they'll have more. They're on the march. To eradicate the trade unions. To eradicate the Communists. To "rid" Europe of the Jewish "race." That's you. And of the Catholics. That's me.

GISA: Of course, I know what they say. But we have other articles in "The Spark." It's about mothers who can't buy milk and the big industrialists who won't implement a fair economic plan.

PAUL: And what about the Nazi plan? Where do you think the Nazis get their money? I went to their rally. 100,000 people. Flags waving. March tunes. Speeches about the righteous place of Germans. Using *our* words of "freedom and bread." And the people in the crowd - I know them. They're like my father. They feel something has been taken from them, are full of spit and fire. My father thrashed out his bitterness at home - I have scars to show for it. These men are hunting for scapegoats. Two marks and a uniform, and they'll march where they're told and attack any who stand in their way. And it's getting worse every day.

GISA: Of course, we all have eyes and ears.

PAUL: So there's something more that you're not telling me. You can't keep it inside. Or you'll burst.

> ADRIANA:
> Or you will burst.
> These voices, these people.
> The peril, the plot.
> The sideways glances.
> The smiles that disappear.

GISA: There was a woman at the bottle plant. Maddalen.

GISA enters into a different place, mentally and physically, as she describes the scene. A woman enters, who is MADDALEN.

GISA: Maddalen does the work of a man, loading and unloading our carts. I thank her when she unloads my cart and she always looks surprised.

MADDALEN gives GISA a note; GISA nods, pockets it.

GISA: One day, she slips me a note with an address. It says "Dinner." I admit I'm pleased to make a friend at the factory. After work, I meet her at the door and we walk along.

GISA and MADDALEN, coats on, walk.

GISA: She says her boyfriend wants to meet the woman who says thank you and is talking about the union. We go to a dismal little building and a tiny apartment. The boyfriend is already there.

THEY enter a room; A MAN greets them.

MADDALEN'S BOYFRIEND: So this is the friend to my Maddalen?

GISA: He points me to a stuffed chair, although most of the stuffing has fallen out. I relax, but perhaps I shouldn't. Things first go badly when he holds up a bottle to pour a glass. I shake my head, but I don't want to explain the ISK rule about drink. Maddalen is at the stove and he calls to her.

MADDALEN'S BOYFRIEND: She doesn't want our wine.

GISA: Maddalen says nothing, so I believe she understands. Soon Maddalen puts a dish on the table—carefully made: stewed, beans, pears—and bacon. I know it has a taste of pork, but I break the rules and eat, heartily.

THEY eat, drink, talk.

GISA: Conversation isn't easy, but it occurs—jobs at the enamel factory, the circus in the park.

As they drain the bottle, Maddalen pokes her boyfriend.

MADDALEN: At least we know she isn't a Jew. A Jew wouldn't eat the bacon!

GISA: This is a joke and they both laugh. Should I let the moment pass? My mind flashes to the day when my sister Ruthie came home, crying, because the teacher made her bow her head to see if she had horns. Finally, I say: "My family is Jewish, although my father will tell anyone who listens that I fail miserably in living up to religious standards." Maddalen yanks away my bowl.

MADDALEN: Judin! No wonder she wouldn't drink our wine.

MADDALEN'S BOYFRIEND: You see what they mean, Maddalen. You see?

GISA: It's a fog, but I gather myself and find my way to the alley.

GISA gets up, nods, leaves.

GISA: The next day when Maddalen unloads my cart, I say "Thank you" as usual. But now I only see blazes behind her eyes.

PAUL: *Gently.* The atmosphere is poisoned. Now the Nazis are stocking real munitions. That's what I found out. And buying them with help from industrialists. What will it say about us if we do nothing? *GISA sits quietly.* I'm not too proud to admit I need help. When we finish, I'll show you how we wash over our troubles with a swim in the Alster. No disputations.

GISA: Promise you won't remind me that I played the fool?

PAUL: You have my word.

GISA and PAUL lean together to write vigorously.

> ADRIANA: *In the MUNICH station.*
> Scars.
> So many scars.
> "To live in the light
> My first skin is made out of leather
> But my second is made out of steel."

ADRIANA stands, turns around.

> GISA: *Speaking to ADRIANA.*
> Wait.
> You must wait.
> DO you HEAR me!
> Please.

> ADRIANA:
> We must wait. We must wait.
> My first of leather. My second of steel.

ADRIANA sits back down.

Scene 10: Hamburg, At the Water, 1930.

GISA and PAUL are swimming outdoors.

PAUL: Dive down. Like this.

GISA: You can dive. I prefer to float on my back and study the sky.

PAUL: The water never holds me up. But, diving down...

GISA: Paul....!

PAUL: I'm sorry — no disputations. You float; I'll dive. *PAUL watches her, as she gently swings her arms.* You're beautiful, Gisa Peiper. Beautiful when you float.

GISA: At school, they all laughed at me when it came to sports.

PAUL: They were wrong.

HE moves to kiss her; SHE lets him and then shies away.

GISA: You were going to dive, as I recall.

Scene 11: Hamburg, ISK headquarters, 1930.

HILDE stands in the ISK headquarters, pulling papers off the Gestetner. WILLIE EICHLER, coat on, stands nearby, reading a copy. HE points to something, reads on.

WILLIE: Excellent work. You need to double the run. Our numbers are growing.

WILLIE takes some copies, puts them under his coat and exits as GISA enters. HE nods to her.

GISA: Hello.

HILDE: Willie read the entire newsletter!

GISA picks a newsletter up from the Gestetner.

GISA: There's a big blob of ink on the front.

HILDE: He's taking some to Berlin. And we're distributing them to dockworkers walking through the ElbeTunnel, first thing in the morning.

GISA: Did he say anything about this blob of ink?

HILDE: Start folding, Gisa. *HILDE imitates WILLIE reading the newsletter aloud.* "'Instead of ending operations when the Nazi party was banned for a year in 1924, the Brown Shirts continued in ocret...' 'Ocret?' Ahh, it's a blob of ink from your machine! 'Continued in secret!'"

GISA: *Now folding newsletters.* Did he complain that I left out the part about the Nazis trying to stage a coup in Bavaria? With the Brown Shirts waving guns while Hitler ran in front of the officials and started screaming, 'Silent!'

HILDE: *Pretending to be WILLIE.* "Good. Skips all that Bavaria mess about why they were banned and gets straight to the point. 'The new unit, called Schutzstaffel or SS, is modeled after Italian fascists and will wear black caps with a 'death's head' symbol. The Nazis are secretly amassing weapons and training as a violent private militia.' Excellent work. You'll need to double the run. Our numbers are growing." *TO GISA.* Fold them in thirds so you can stuff them up your sleeve.

GISA: You and Paul are handling distribution, right?

HILDE: All hands on deck. And you need to use precautions when we go to the ElbeTunnel. You never know where a Brown Shirt is lurking.

GISA: I'm to be at my new job at the nail factory before the bell to collect union pledges.

HILDE: Franz was followed by two goons the other day until he dropped into a market and slipped behind the potato bins - and some very large shoppers. My cousin's boyfriend says Brown Shirts are secretly everywhere - even in the police.

GISA: That's criminal.

HILDE: If they knock on your door, it's a warning, even if they say nothing. They're watching you! So stuff them up your sleeve. Pretend you're looking for a friend. Then pull a newsletter out when a dockworker signals that he's interested with a nod of his head.

HILDE demonstrates.

GISA: I'm not good at pretending.

HILDE: Try it.

HILDE stuffs newsletters up GISA's sleeves. GISA tries getting one out, but gets stuck.

>ADRIANA: *(Munich Station)*
>There is time, and yet there is time
>When the world lies ahead
>When the world lets us dream.
>Make haste, make haste.
>For these times are not ours to keep.

HILDE: Now I'm Max, the dockworker, and when I nod — you slip one out... And don't gawk at the dockworker like he's Paul.

SHE walks along, in imitation of a dockworker.

GISA: It's tangled. I don't gawk at Paul. And anyhow, who 'gawks' at Franz?

HILDE: Franz and I work together on committees. Maybe, I like him. A little.

GISA: Everything with Paul is an argument.

HILDE: I'm sure you win.

GISA: Not always.

HILDE: I've known Paul since we raced by the lake with mud between our toes. He'd argue with a toad, if the toad gave him a chance. But when Paul is leading hikes, I see a dimple on your cheek.

GISA fixes her sleeve, and adjusts her clothing.

GISA: I'm sure I'm studying bird life. My sleeve isn't big enough.

HILDE: Well, don't gawk at the stevedore like you gawk at the... birds.

Grabbing a newsletter, HILDE imitates a dockworker. "Ach, Nazis, Nazis. You come and live with me and I'll protect you from those big bad wolves." *GISA AND HILDE laugh. HILDE studies newsletter.* Willie was very impressed. Thinks you should take up teaching.

GISA: Tutoring is enough for me.

HILDE: Hamburg University is starting free courses.

GISA: And I'm doing better at organizing workers at my new job.... did I tell you? I think we have a good chance of winning an hourly raise.

> ADRIANA: *(Munich Station.)*
> Follow the steps.
> Listen to what they tell you.
> Say nothing. Pretend.
> You'll soon be on your way.
> Follow the steps.

HILDE: Don't you think the workers want good teachers for their children?

PAUL enters with his bicycle.

PAUL: Sorry. Had a flat tire.

HILDE: We're finished now. All folded, ready to go.

PAUL: Then you and I will meet early. You can do the walkway inside the tunnel, I'll do the outside.

GISA: And me.

PAUL: It's not the kind of thing you want to do. After all, you're the editor.

GISA: What? You think I can't play the part? All hands on deck.

SHE demonstrates pulling out a newsletter from her sleeve, hands it to PAUL.

GISA: One, two... your newsletter, and I walk on.

PAUL: "The Nazis are arming! This has to end! How can I help?"

HILDE: You're right, sir! We must stop them!

PAUL: We will!

GISA: We shall.

Scene 12. Munich Train Station, 1938.

>ADRIANA:
>Learn and tell.
>Study and teach.
>Learn and tell!
>Study and teach!
>
>PAUL: *His voice is heard, but he cannot be seen.*
>Life I wrote on my banner.
>
>ADRIANA:
>Where are you? Paul?
>... My skin, of leather. My skin, of steel. My skin.

Scene 13: Hamburg, ISK Headquarters, 1930.

After distributing newsletters at the ElbeTunnel, GISA and HILDE return to the ISK headquarters.

HILDE: The door's not closed properly.

As the door opens, THEY see PAUL, sprawled on the floor. GISA starts to run over; HILDE stops her.

GISA: *SHE turns from PAUL to HILDE and back to PAUL.* Paul. He's hurt! They attacked you?

PAUL: Leave me alone.

GISA: Are you bleeding?

PAUL: I'm not bleeding.

HILDE: Why are you lying on the floor? Aren't you going to work?

PAUL: So I can make a fancy car interior for some rich person? Carve his initials on the dashboard? Why? Those dockworkers don't care. "'The Spark.' You must mean that redhead in the beer hall! Ha ha, ha." Two of them actually sneered. One said: "We'll take the Nazis over the likes of you."

GISA: That's one person.

PAUL: TWO.

HILDE: One dockworker thanked me.

PAUL: And then what? Into the dustbin?

HILDE: You're drunk, aren't you?

PAUL: What if I am?

HILDE: You know it's against the rules.

PAUL: I don't care about the rules. Or Willie Eichler or Minna Specht, or what they think of me.

GISA: Well, I'm glad you asked me to help write your article. If you're too blind to understand that we're doing what we can, then you should stop going around saying that you have a skin of leather and a skin of steel. You have a skin of gooseberries and glass. It's a waste.

PAUL: And what about you... won't apply to the university! Hilde told me!

GISA: I'm going to work. He can sulk on his own.

GISA leaves.

HILDE: I won't tell, Paul. You're my oldest friend. But if you aren't

46 Silence Not A Love Story

part of the ISK, I don't want to be part of it, either.

HILDE exits, but as she does so, GISA returns.

GISA: And another thing, don't forget your tutoring lesson. Your appearance is expected, Friday, promptly on time, and with all assignments complete.

GISA exits again, leaving PAUL. She returns again.

Be early.

> ADRIANA: *(Munich Station)*
> "In us lives a will, good and clear.
> We do not cry any more - yet we stroke
> softly the brow and hair of another who was hurt."
>
> A poem. Put it in a poem.
> In a sculpture. In an etching.
>
> Mend the broken.
> Touch the scars.
> Stroke the hurt.

Scene 14: Hamburg, Gisa's Room, 1930.

PAUL waits for GISA at her room. SHE rushes in.

GISA: The lesson plan has changed.

PAUL: Oh?

GISA: From now on, I need to manage my time very carefully. Especially since I'm starting classes.

PAUL: Classes? At the university?

GISA: I happened to apply. And they responded. First line: "Admission granted." Second line: Classes begin next week.

PAUL: That's good news.

GISA: I barely have time to adjust.

PAUL: You don't have to worry about tutoring me.

GISA: You don't want to learn?

PAUL turns to leave.

PAUL: Another tutor will come along.

GISA: If it makes no difference to you, fine — I'll use the time for a paying position.

PAUL: *Exiting.* Very well. I'll see you at the next ISK meeting.

GISA steps in front of PAUL and blocks him.

GISA: I could use some help.

I need a frame. For my Käthe Kollwitz prints. I need a frame that stands like steel, but doesn't put holes into Frieda's walls.

GISA pulls out her folder with the Kollwitz prints. SHE takes out one in particular.

PAUL: *HE studies the print.* "Never Again War." It's as if you can rub off the charcoal from the paper.

GISA: After making it, she wrote: "Everyone must work as she can... to be effective in this time."

PAUL: Yes, she's in a position to do that — a well-known professor; her husband, a doctor.

GISA: She found a purpose. To serve a greater cause. With her art. That's what she meant when she said: "Remember this also when you are old."

PAUL: Are you lecturing me?

HE turns to leave again. GISA stands in front of him, blocking him.

GISA: I'm talking about myself. Art helps me survive. Teaching will be my art and these prints will remind me of why I do what I do when times are hard. *SHE pauses.* If you help with a frame, I'll pay you back in tutoring time.

PAUL stands mute. GISA starts wrapping up her prints.

I don't know why I bothered. I thought you'd understand what it means to be true to what you believe.

PAUL: *Stops her from packing away the prints.* I can give you a frame.

GISA: I don't want "a frame." I want a sturdy frame.

PAUL: I can give you a sturdy frame. A frame worthy of Kollwitz.

GISA: *Puts her hand on his heart.* I need a frame that can stand the test of time, one that will hold up against bumps and tears.

PAUL: You have my word. I promise. *(HE pauses a moment.)* But don't expect that there will be "no disputations." I am a man with disputations.

GISA: Don't expect that you'll win your disputations. You'll have to learn to live with losing them.

PAUL: No. I don't think so. I don't plan to lose them. You're wrong on that one.

GISA: Then, I'll agree to lose — occasionally. *(SHE pauses.)* To life, Paul, to life.

THEY sink into one another.

Scene 15. Munich Train Station, 1938.

ADRIANA:
White clouds grow into the air
Like mountains rising baseless from blue lakes.
Banks, wooded, dissolve in light,
Their dusky shadows sunk in fragrant blue.

Sun, Light, Strength.
Life. Life and youth.

The strength we feel in us to fight
against everything dark and weak.

Mend the broken.
Stroke the hurt.

There is poetry,
There is art.

There are disputations to be had.

Scene 16: Hamburg, Gisa's Room, 1932.

FRIEDA knocks on the door of GISA's room.

FRIEDA: Gisa, answer! You remember, we're dancing tonight? It's bad enough that you pay the rent in pennies, but not to show up as promised? I don't want to leave Lilla alone.

GISA walks in behind FRIEDA.

GISA: Here I am.

>ADRIANA: *At the Munich station, calling to GISA, across time and space.*
>Where are we?
>
>GISA: *To ADRIANA.* At the landlady's. At Frieda's. You know that.
>
>ADRIANA: But when?
>
>GISA: Why must you ask? You know the answer. 1932.
>
>ADRIANA: 1932? There's time, then. There is still time.

A SOLDIER in the train station walks by ADRIANA. SHE acknowledges him, then closes her eyes as if sleeping.

ADRIANA: Life I wrote on my banner.

FRIEDA: I was about to give up.

GISA: I had lessons with the neighborhood children.

FRIEDA: And you were in the library, no doubt. With the stack of books you've piled up here, maybe you plan to start a library in my apartment.

GISA: You're welcome to borrow them.

FRIEDA: And what? Have them banging on my door every day?

ADRIANA: *In the Munich station.* Is this the beginning? Is this the end of time?

GISA: Who?

FRIEDA: Who? Who? Do you think I know who they are? Men! *SHE whispers.* How do you think it looks to my neighbors to have police at my door?

GISA: The police?

FRIEDA: They didn't have uniforms. Only badges.

GISA: Did you let them in?

FRIEDA: I don't know what these books are. Suppose they're... dangerous.

GISA: A book... is a book. A book can't be dangerous.

FRIEDA: They insisted on looking.

GISA: At my papers? At what?

FRIEDA: The room. They looked at the room and made notes. I said you weren't available because you promised to sit and this is the big dance competition. After that, they left.

GISA: I see. *GISA looks around the room, distracted.* Very well, then. Tell Lilla to come over.

FRIEDA exits. As soon as she exits, GISA frantically begins going through her books, and looking to see if anything is missing. SHE checks a framed Kollwitz, looks behind it, under it.

ADRIANA: Did she call them? Why did they come? Is she the one? Did she tell them some thing?

GISA closes the door, pulls a piece of paper from under her dress, and then puts the paper in her mouth and eats it. FRIEDA knocks again.

GISA: One minute. *GISA swallows, drinks water, then opens the door.*

FRIEDA: Do you like my dress?

GISA: Fringes? Very cosmopolitan.

FRIEDA: *She speaks quietly.* They had Hilde's name on the list, too. I saw it.

GISA: What did they want?

FRIEDA: You can't ask too many questions. I'm only me. Don't make it so difficult.

SHE twirls around.

Wish me luck.

GISA: Yes, I do.

ADRIANA: Don't make it so difficult.

Scene 17. Hamburg, ISK Headquarters, 1932.

At the ISK headquarters. PAUL carves a woodblock for a poster. An older man, MENDEL, in mild disarray, comes to the entry.

MENDEL: This is what left wing political clubs look like? Right in the Reeperbahn? With sex shops all around?

PAUL: It's what this one looks like.

MENDEL: Where are all the big banners and flags? "Fair wages for all!" Rah rah rah.

> ADRIANA: *SHE speaks to GISA, who stands to the side and watches this scene as well.* I don't want to remember. Stop now.
>
> GISA: *SHE speaks back to ADRIANA.* I can't stop it.
>
> ADRIANA: You weren't there.
>
> GISA: I heard the story; I know the story.
>
> ADRIANA: Let's find something else. I don't want to remember. Stop.

PAUL addresses the man, who has now entered and is roaming throughout the ISK offices.

PAUL: I don't want any trouble, right?

MENDEL: As I suspected. Nothing to say for yourself. *MENDEL picks up a sample from the woodcut.* Simple-minded, if you ask me.

PAUL: It makes a point about the upcoming election. We can turn the tide.

MENDEL: Fools. Watch them march and scream for the "fatherland," and throw rocks under the wheel of your wagon, and laugh when it breaks. You can't stop them.

PAUL: We can change the direction. We're going to every beer hall in Hamburg before the election to speak to the people.

MENDEL: Who can even count the number of elections in the last year? One crook goes, and another is put in. Two months later, another election, another group of crooks. What rubbish. How much did the crooks in the Reichstag lose when the banks closed last summer? Not a penny, I guarantee you. People would be happy for a job, people would be happy for customers to come to their bakery. This is what makes a nice girl leave her family in Berlin and come to work in some sleazy place with whorehouses all around?

>   ADRIANA: *Shouting across time to MENDEL in the other scene; he doesn't hear.*
>   Stop now. Stop. You're going too far.

Then to GISA, who stands watching, wanly, and says nothing.

>   Tell the old man to STOP.

PAUL: So you are Mr. Peiper? Gisa's father? I'm Gerhardt — Gerhardt Paul Konopka.

MENDEL: I don't want to know who you are. Three daughters. And one in this... dump in Hamburg.

PAUL: I can get on my bicycle and find Gisa for you. It would be an honor, sir.

MENDEL: Save your voice, Konopka. We Jews have enough misery.

PAUL: My mother's very fond of Gisa. We have plans...

MENDEL: Misery. And why not? *Der Sturmer*, every week, with another story about the Jewish "infestation" of Europe. I'd be pleased to die. But they destroyed headstones at the Jewish cemetery. You can't even die in peace anymore. Doesn't that amuse you, Konopka?

PAUL: No sir. I must dispute you on that. Three daughters, sir: Ruth into nursing; Hanna to Palestine. Gisa will be a certified teacher in less than a year. If your customers had a decent wage for their labor, they'd be buying your bread.

MENDEL: Maybe he'll make things better. Maybe he'll get a majority in the election and get rid of the criminal element and the terrorists and Communists. Bring back law and order. Maybe that's what we need.

PAUL: You can't believe that? That we should capitulate? Kant said each one of us must act as if he is legislating for the world. As if freedom fell on your deeds. As if you alone had to answer for it. Kant was a great philosopher and he spoke to...

MENDEL: Kant? I don't care about Kant. I came to see my daughter, and I want to make sure you understand this, Konopka: I do not approve of my daughter spending her time with a Catholic. That's all there is to it, Konopka.

PAUL: I'd like to change your mind, sir.

MENDEL: You won't.

Scene 18: Munich Train Station, 1938.

>ADRIANA: *SHE has her head is down as if she is asleep.*
>Too much sorrow.
>Too much pain.

>SOLDIER 1: *He comes over and shakes her.*
>Hey!

>ADRIANA: *SHE sits up and tries to contain her fright.*
>Remember your name.
>Remember the name you have. Remember the name to travel:
>Adriana.

>Sit.
>Don't speak. Don't talk.

SOLDIER 1 seats himself next to her.

> SOLDIER 1: You'll miss your train!

ADRIANA waves her hand in thanks.

> You bet your buttons you can thank me. I'll bet you're getting cold. *He puts his arm around her.* To Anschluss!

> ADRIANA: *She nods her head, as if weary.*

Sit.
Don't cry. Don't laugh.
Sit.
Float.
Float.
Float.

Scene 19. Hamburg, At the Water, 1932.

GISA swims with PAUL, outdoors, in an unspecific location.

GISA: Hold your hands by your side. Look up at the sky. Come on, float, Paul, float. Relax. Let your worries flow into the water.

PAUL: I'm a fool.

GISA: Shhhh.

SHE kisses him on the face, repeatedly.

Shh. Now float with me.

Scene 20. Hamburg, Hilde's Apartment, late 1932.

GISA knocks on a door and calls out.

GISA: Hilde! Time to get to the docks.

HILDE answers the door and is still in nightclothes.

HILDE: It's dark out.

GISA: I'll turn my back so you can get dressed.

HILDE begins to dress.

HILDE: Sometimes I wonder if people in other political clubs are getting up while it's still dark. Why is it only the ISK?

GISA: We have first-hand accounts from Dessau. People will get a taste of what the Nazis have in store for the whole country when they hear what's happened there.

> ADRIANA: *(In the Munich station, calling across time.)*
> Information!
> Information!
> What year?

GISA momentarily leaves the scene with HILDE and sits between SOLDIER 1 and ADRIANA, and looks ADRIANA directly in the eye.

> GISA:
> Hold on. You must hold on..
> You'll be out of Germany again
> and on your way. Soon.
>
> You know the year. 1932. October 1932. The eve of 1933.

THE WOMAN from the first scene, boozy and freewheeling, sits on the SOLDIER'S lap, pushing both GISA and ADRIANA aside. GISA observes this and gets up, going back to her conversation with HILDE. SOLDIER 1 and THE WOMAN eventually leave together and ADRIANA sits alone again.

GISA: *(With her back to HILDE.)* Are you dressing?

HILDE: When will it end? It's already been - what? More than two years since we published the article about the SS. You know what the Communists say?

GISA: You wouldn't trust the Communists if you heard my mother's stories from Poland.

HILDE: I met a very nice Communist at a club last night.

GISA: At a club? And he 'danced' his way into your thoughts? Did he tell you there was no danger of the Nazis gaining ground?

HILDE: He said that it might be best if the Nazis took over and then everyone would see that a revolution is necessary. "Letting the Nazis come to power will pave the way for the workers' paradise."

GISA: You must find someone else to dance with you, Hilde.

HILDE: He wasn't ridiculous and wild.

GISA: Of course, they aren't all like that. My friend Rudy in Berlin is a Communist. He always wears a hat, cocked to the side. *(SHE demonstrates this.)* We'd go to the museums and discuss Holbein. Or Rousseau. He lives in a fancy neighborhood with streets as wide as his smile. We stayed friends even after he fell in with the Communists. He used to say: "Art and friendship is all you need to survive. And we will always have that."

GISA is inexplicably rattled, as if seeing something. SHE suddenly straightens.

But this Communist dancer will lead you to danger, Hilde.

HILDE: The ISK has already led me to danger. What is going to the ElbeTunnel at five in the morning, other than danger?

GISA: Yes, but you are the first to say that we need to keep the dockworkers informed. And they definitely should know what's happened in Dessau. The Nazis shut down the Bauhaus design school. The most famous school of art! Paul Klee. Wassily Kandinsky. You've seen his Wassily chair, right? With strips for the back and the seat instead of an old-fashioned cushion? The Nazis call it "cosmopolitan rubbish." "Degenerate." A chair! They're making all the children join Nazi youth groups, and they're banning a chair! Käthe Kollwitz issued a call to action! When we go to the Tunnel, we're saying it's not too late.

HILDE: The police let me know they're watching. Men came to my mother's house.

GISA now turns to HILDE and faces her.

GISA: We'll follow all of the precautions.

HILDE: My mother's been sick.

GISA: The Nazis recruit every day. Do you know what a girl told me at school last week? "I can always smell a Jew and, when I do, I get up and walk as far as I can in the other direction." So I said, "It's a surprise, then, that you're sitting next to me." (SHE laughs.) This is what that Communist dancer says is not a problem.

HILDE: That's not it, Gisa. I'm not brave. I can't swim. I don't do well under pressure.

GISA: What are you telling me? Someone said you're better off not to be seen by the Tunnel with a Jew at five in the morning?

HILDE: I'm saying... my mother isn't well. Spitting up blood. I have three brothers, one sister: all younger. Someone must look after them, mustn't someone?

GISA: You don't have to say any more, Hilde. I can meet the dockworkers on my own.

GISA starts to leave, then turns back.

I understand, dear Hilde. You're very much in my heart. I understand.

GISA leaves.

    ADRIANA:
Once we held each other in a close circle.
Stood linked.
Friends.
Allies.
Family.

Once we held each other close.
The world was outside.
The world was outside and we had to let go.
We had to let go.
Now breathe.
Breathe.

Breathe.

Once again the dark pressure will lift.
The streets will be beautiful.
Breathe
Breathe.
The sky will open wide.
The nightmare will lift from the soul.
Breathe.
Breathe.
Now breathe.

END OF ACT ONE

ACT TWO

Scene 1. Munich Train Station, 1938.

> ADRIANA:
> Softly stands the night before my heart
> I am not afraid
> and nothing hurts.
> Over all the dark suffering
> lies calm
> like a deep sea.

SOLDIER 1 and SOLDIER 2 in the MUNICH station become boisterous. THE WOMAN pours more beers and when they grab her, SHE goes along with them. As earlier, THE WOMAN pays close attention to ADRIANA.

> SOLDIERS: *Singing.*
> "The flag high! The ranks tightly closed!
> Clear the street for the brown battalions...

> ADRIANA: *Overlapping the soldiers.*
> Over all the dark suffering
> Over all the dark suffering
> I am not afraid.

> SOLDIERS & THE WOMAN:
> ... Clear the street for the SA man!"

> ADRIANA:
> Art and friendship.
> We will always
> Have that.

Silence Not A Love Story

Scene 2: Hamburg, A Cemetery, 1933.

FRANZ stands in a winter coat before a gravestone in a cemetery. PAUL and GISA walk up. GISA reads the stone and puts a pebble on top of it.

GISA: K-o-h-l. Kohl. Is it someone we know? Died in 1929 — that's 4 years ago.

PAUL addresses FRANZ.

PAUL: The message said "urgent." Gisa's exams are coming up in a matter of hours.

> ADRIANA: *She speaks across time from a different place.*
> Oh. I remember.
> February. Cold February.
> Bone chilling February.
> 1933 February.
> The February to end February.

GISA: Don't worry about me.

FRANZ: This wasn't my idea. I have such a headache, same as at the shop when the ink soaks into your hair and starts running in your blood.

GISA: We're all sick with the news. Let's hurry before we freeze to death and end up in one of these holes. Why torture ourselves?

> ADRIANA:
> Why torture ourselves?
> Why do this?

> GISA: *Speaking to ADRIANA.*
> I didn't mean torture, torture;
> It was a turn of the tongue.

> ADRIANA:
> Torture is not a turn of the tongue.

---

62   Silence Not A Love Story

GISA:
You mustn't think about these things.
Just sit.

ADRIANA:
Just sit.
I am sitting.
Just sit.

FRANZ: Right. So here it is: Our headquarters are gone. Vandalized. Ransacked. One of the "ladies" next door saved the Gestetner and this.

FRANZ pulls out a broken piece of wood from his jacket.

PAUL: Bastards!

GISA: We'll rebuild. That won't stop us.

PAUL: Right. They do whatever they want! Ignore the law. Or change the law so that the law isn't the law, but a perversion of the law, and the things that decent people do are illegal. What did the stupid old fool who sits as president think would happen when he invited Hitler to be part of his government? To be his 'Chancellor?' Before we were fighting one party. Now, three days later, they're in power. And — this.

GISA: Willie and Minna will help.

FRANZ: I'm not so sure about the ISK anymore. Pacifism isn't getting us anywhere. Maybe we should be arming.

PAUL: Stop! We'll manage. People in Hamburg won't stand for this. This is a labor town.

FRANZ: I suppose. *HE pauses.* There's more. Willie and Minna are going to Paris. They'll set up safe houses for anti-Nazi exiles; work to get other nations to intervene and bring this to a fast end.

GISA: They're leaving?

ADRIANA:
Some people are leaving.
Do you remember?

In February.
The days after. The weeks after.
Why didn't you think about leaving?

GISA:
I'm not prepared to leave.

ADRIANA:
Some people are leaving.
You could have left then.
Some people are leaving.

GISA:
I have my mother.
I have children to tutor.
I have school.
I'll be working in a classroom soon.
Education can change everything.

ADRIANA:
You're a foolish girl.
You'll end up in prison.
You'll end up in a camp.
You'll end up...

GISA:
Quiet. I'm not prepared to leave.
We can do things.

FRANZ: And all political rallies are banned. Except the Nazis.

PAUL: We'll go underground. We're prepared for this. We beat them back in the last election; we can beat them back again. It'll be better being underground.

GISA: It won't be better.

PAUL: We can do things. We'll learn to be more clever than they are.

FRANZ: The word from Berlin is that they've already set up barracks out in the country where they take people.

GISA: People? What people?

FRANZ: People. I don't know. Dissidents. People they don't like. Communists, I guess.

GISA: Who's been taken? On what grounds? We need to get a list.

PAUL: I'm sure it's all whispers and rumors. That's how these people think. It builds up fear, and that's what they want.

GISA: We need to start publishing the names of people who are missing.

FRANZ: Forget the names. Especially if the police come, you must forget all the names you know. Practice forgetting so that the only thing you remember is that you remember nothing, and if you do remember something, you must pretend not to know, you must remember only to lie about it.

> ADRIANA:
> You must remember nothing.
> You must remember to lie about it.

GISA: "Remember to lie." We've spent years getting out the truth. And now, we must lie?

PAUL: You're not questioning that, are you?

GISA: Only you can question things?

PAUL: That kind of questioning will open a fissure that can't be mended. We'll tell as much of the truth as we can. As long as it hurts to lie, you're safe.

GISA: Then I'll be very safe. *She pauses a moment.* I'd like to go now.

FRANZ: Wait. There's more. Anyone who's stopped by the Gestapo must be cut off. We'll assume that they're being used as bait and followed. There will be no new ISK members.

GISA: And what of former members?

FRANZ: No communications. No conversations. No encounters.

PAUL: Except...

FRANZ: No exceptions. Including Hilde.

PAUL: We're neighbors... we grew up together...

FRANZ: Now she must be a stranger. If arrested, she'll be pressed for names.

PAUL: But Hilde's mother and my mother...

FRANZ: Then you must make your mother a stranger.

PAUL: I take care of my mother!

GISA: Surely, there can be an exception for his mother, Franz. Can't we agree on that?

FRANZ: Times have changed. My parents put in to the Jewish board for visas. I told them — if something comes through, I'm not going. We'll all be sorry if we don't extricate ourselves from entanglements.

PAUL: My mother is not an entanglement! And if you want to talk about entanglements, you and Hilde are not exactly strangers!

FRANZ: Anything between us is over.

GISA: Very well, then. None of us will be in contact with Hilde.

PAUL tosses down woodcut he's been holding.

PAUL: I'm through with the ISK! Make your own damn posters!

PAUL starts to leave. GISA blocks his path.

GISA: You will not leave like that, Gerhardt Paul Konopka.

FRANZ: Listen, Paul: Take care of your mother. DON'T TALK to her about the ISK!

GISA: That's fair.

PAUL: Don't speak for me, Gisa. No one has a right to monitor how I talk to my mother!

FRANZ: Your honor is our insurance. *FRANZ picks woodcut, hands it back to PAUL.*

Please... my head is splitting. *FRANZ starts to leave.*

PAUL: *HE grabs FRANZ and clasps his hand.* Wish Gisa well on her exams.

FRANZ: Yes. I do.

We're in the middle of something we don't even know.

FRANZ leaves; PAUL kneels; then HE and GISA depart.

>ADRIANA: *(At the Munich Station.)*
>That won't stop us.
>No.
>They won't stop us.
>No.
>Won't stop us.

Scene 3. Hamburg, Gisa's Room, 1933.

Immediately after the meeting in the cemetery, GISA enters her room. Everything is in disarray. SHE searches frantically for books and papers.

GISA: My books! My notes for the exam! Who's been in here? Lilla? Frieda? Who let them in? Where are my books! My books are not dangerous!

GISA collapses, astonished. And then sees her framed Käthe Kollwitz print. SHE picks it up and grasps it to her chest, clearly shaken and emotional.

GISA: Art and friendship. Remember this also when you are old.

Scene 4. Berlin, A Bakery/Apartment, 1933.

GISA enters her father's bakery in Berlin, which also doubles as her family's apartment. SHE starts searching through the room, opening cupboards and boxes. BRONIA, GISA'S mother, enters, coming from behind a curtain that is pulled across part of the room.

BRONIA: Gisela!

GISA: Mother! Why isn't there any bread?

BRONIA: *SHE points to the space behind the curtain.* Your father's taking a rest. We decided not to bake today.

GISA: Where are the leftovers?

BRONIA: We rested yesterday, as well.

GISA: How long has this been going on?

> ADRIANA:
> You must remember nothing.
> Don't think.
> Don't smile.
> Don't laugh.
>
> Remember a poem.
> Else Lasker-Schuler.
> 'I have a blue piano at home
> yet I don't know a single tune.'

BRONIA: Passover will be here soon, and people will want matzoh instead of bread.

GISA: Passover's in April — over a month away.

BRONIA: Talk to him, Gisela.

GISA moves behind a curtain, which is another room where MENDEL lies.

GISA: Papa?

MENDEL: Oh, she's descended from the throne to come and visit. I hope you didn't waste all your money to travel here.

At the Munich Train Station, SOLDIER 2 walks up to ADRIANA. He is slightly drunk.

    SOLDIER 2: Hey lady. Are you where you're supposed to be?

ADRIANA *nods.*

    SOLDIER 2: Good, then. Good for you, lady! *HE sits by her.* Time moves so fast. The trains are moving faster than ever. Trains are moving faster than time. Like a riddle! Five years ago, I was in the Youth Corps. But I knew it wouldn't be long!
    Oh, I see you have a wedding ring. I hope I'm not intruding.

SOLDIER 2 takes ADRIANA's hand. ADRIANA shakes her head and tries to ease her hand away.

GISA: *SHE talks to her father in a curtained off part of their bakery/apartment in Berlin.*

I finished my exams last month. I'll be a teacher soon. Have you seen a doctor?

MENDEL: Did you bring that Catholic with you?

GISA: Then you haven't seen a doctor?

    SOLDIER 2: *HE talks to ADRIANA at the MUNICH station.* Here's a game I play with the new men: Where were you on February 27, 1933? Then I tell them: On February 27 when I heard that Communists lit fire to our Reichstag building, I traded in my short pants. And in only five years: union with Austria!

ADRIANA shakes her head; the SOLDIER puts her hand down.

SOLDIER 2: You must have come off the train from Vienna... waiting for the Paris connection. *ADRIANA nods lightly.* Before today, an Austrian can be forgiven for not remembering February 27, 1933. But after today, you'll have me to thank.

Semi-oblivious to her, SOLDIER 2 hums a bit of the Horst Wessel song, sleepily gets up and walks away.

MENDEL: I don't need a doctor. I can end this quickly. Served in the Great War; what thanks do I get? If I had my gun, I could put a gravestone at my head. Are you still part of that group of agitators?

GISA: Group? No. I'm not in any group.

MENDEL: Don't lie to me, Gisela. A daughter who lies is good for nothing.

GISA: I don't want to argue.

MENDEL: You're with some left-wing group that has an office in the sex quarter and tells you to lie to your father! *HE calls out.* Bronia! Mother!

GISA: I'd like to say the evening prayer with you.

MENDEL: Another lie. The Rebbe should hear the way you burn my ears! When did you last observe Shabbes? Not in years.

GISA: And then we can think about a place where you can take a mineral bath and get a cure.

MENDEL: I don't need that nonsense. Hah. Bronia! Where is the note? After Mother informs you about your friend, we can talk mineral baths and cures and other lies.

BRONIA: *She enters the same area.* Shhh. You will never get better.

GISA: What friend?

MENDEL: Show her the note! That Communist boy.

GISA: Rudy? I'm planning to visit him.

BRONIA: Oh no, you can't do that.

MENDEL: Rich boy and a Communist, too. Ha ha. What a joke. A boy who 'likes' boys and a Communist, too. He's the one who gave her the prints of that fanatical artist.

GISA: Käthe Kollwitz. You can't talk about her like that.

MENDEL: Oh yes I can! University let her go! Ha ha. Now she's a victim, too. That's what we Jews do best: suffer. Show her the note, Bronia!

BRONIA: I'm not sure what happened to it.

GISA: No one mentioned it.

BRONIA: I was packing the deliveries when some fellow brought it by. I put it away.

GISA: It must be in your apron.

GISA goes to the other room, begins opening drawers wildly, whipping out aprons.

BRONIA follows GISA, closing the drawers GISA opens.

BRONIA: I may have lost it. With your sisters gone, it's too hard to keep everything together.

BRONIA takes GISA by the arm. Come, Gisa, say the evening prayers with your father.

GISA: *SHE resists BRONIA, keeps searching.* I don't want to any more.

BRONIA: The note was nothing. A birthday greeting, possibly.

GISA: You read it?

BRONIA: Of course not.

GISA: Then how do you know what it said?

BRONIA: Stop interrogating me, Gisela!

GISA: I'll go to their house and find out.

BRONIA: *Confidentially so MENDEL does not hear.* We hear things. We hear stories. We hear rumors. People are not always where they are supposed to be.

GISA: What are you saying?

BRONIA: Shops closing, people packing in the night. Doors kicked open. The fire — the Reichstag fire. We hear stories.

GISA: We can stop them. It's not too late.

BRONIA: They're saying it was Communists who started the fire. *Whispering.*

But if you ask me, the SS lit the match so they could bang on doors and bully people and ship them off to God-knows where.

GISA: Are you saying that's what happened to Rudy? Mother?

BRONIA: Please, Gisa, don't bring danger. You know what your father has? Melancholy, that's what. Can't you be a good girl?

> ADRIANA: *She speaks across time to GISA.* Be a good girl. Come sit with me.
> I won't look so alone if you sit with me.
> I won't have to lie if you sit with me.

> GISA:
> You're going crazy.
> Gather your senses.

> ADRIANA:
> I remember.
> This much, I remember.

Scene 5. Hamburg Train Station, 1933.

GISA exits a train in the Hamburg station, not unlike the beginning of the play. GISA looks around and HILDE rushes in, grabs her and swirls her around.

HILDE: Gisa! Hello! What a wonderful surprise to see you here! Are you in from Berlin?

GISA: *Pulling away.* I'm not feeling well. You probably shouldn't get too close.

HILDE: But I must tell you my news! I'm engaged! His name is Renne... from Belgium.

GISA: Yes-very well—congratulations—I really must go. Nauseous.

PAUL: *Enters without seeing HILDE, and strides toward GISA.* At last! Three weeks seemed like...

HILDE: *Turns to PAUL.* Paul, there you are. You've been such a stranger.

PAUL: Hiking a lot. In the woods. Up in Blankensee.

HILDE: Renne and I would love to go hiking. My mother must have mentioned Renne...?

PAUL: Yes, good news, then. *HE takes GISA's arm and addresses her.* We'd best be going, right?

HILDE: She's not well. *SHE takes GISA's other arm.* Here, let me accompany you to the latrine. I'm early for meeting Renne's mother...

GISA/PAUL: *Simultaneously.* No, I'll (she'll) be okay. Thank you.

PAUL moves GISA away and they exit abruptly.

HILDE: Nice seeing you. Nice seeing old... friends....

Scene 6: Munich Train Station, 1938.

>ADRIANA:
This is a poem
Not a prayer.
This is a promise
Not a song.

This is from me to you,
both in ragged brown.
You, unknown, in the yard.
Me, unseen, peeking through bars.

You, at the butt of guns
'Run boy run.' 'Stand.'
'Sit.' 'Roll over.' 'Jump.'
'Faster, boy.' 'Faster.' 'Faster, boy.' 'Faster.'

I see the blood fill your mouth.
I see red pour from your nose.
I see you stumble and fall.
I see no monument for your crown.

Your last hot breath sears the air,
burnishes steel beneath my gown.
I am your witness
And this is not a prayer.

>GISA:
When is that?
Where?

>ADRIANA:
You don't want to know.
It is nothing you want to know.

Scene 7: Hamburg, University Offices, 1933.

GISA knocks again and again at the door of an office at her college in Hamburg. No one answers. A man, PROF. KALTENBACH, grabs her and pulls her away.

PROF. KALTENBACH: Come come come, Miss Peiper, to my office.

GISA: I'm looking for Professor Blumenthal. He's the reviewer on my dissertation.

PROF. KALTENBACH: I don't want you to worry— our prize pupil in the education department! Everything will be fine.

GISA: What do you mean?

PROF. KALTENBACH: I will assess in Blumenthal's place.

GISA: But Professor Blumenthal...?

PROF. KALTENBACH:... has advised me where I can find all his notes on... on...

GISA:... reforming the authoritarian structure of the lower grades.

PROF. KALTENBACH: I'll do my best to pick up. The decision was handed down. New employment rules, new civil service rules.

GISA: Prof. Blumenthal is gone? With the snap of a finger? What jobs will there be for me?

PROF. KALTENBACH: Surely, there's a hole in the system to accommodate you.

GISA: *SHE sees and picks up a picture of Hitler from his desk.* You think they'll bend? You add a picture to your desk, a button to your lapel, reshape your views? How can you?

PROF. KALTENBACH: *He fingers and covers a swastika on his lapel.* One must make a living. One must carry on. One must live within the times.

GISA: Then what must you think of me?

SHE drops the photo face down and exits.

PROF. KALTENBACH: *Calling GISA.* Miss Peiper, please... I want to help you.

Scene 8: Hamburg, At the Water, 1933.

    ADRIANA: *SHE speaks across time from the Munich Station.*
Poetry and art.
A dip in clear water.
A sunrise when a window is opened
behind a prison wall.
Remember.
There is some good.

In Hamburg, GISA and PAUL are at the Alster Lake. SHE stands in the water, he lies in it.

PAUL: See how my floating's improved.

GISA: Your legs are dangling. You need to be flat.

PAUL: You're very tough.

GISA: Float with your head toward the sky while I dive down.

PAUL: No.

GISA: That's how you'll improve.

PAUL: I'm going to watch you dive.

GISA: As if I were a child?

PAUL: As if I knew you filled your cuffs and fists with rocks.

PAUL reaches and pulls a rock from her swim clothes.

What's this?

GISA: It would be better if I could disappear.

PAUL: *Fiercely, he pulls out rocks in her suit and clothes and tosses them away.*

Do you think you're fighting this alone? Am I any less attacked because I'm not Jewish? We're all in this together! If you and I don't have the courage to resist, then who will?

GISA: I'm... tired.

PAUL: Then listen to the ripples in the lake. Then write a poem. Then sing a song. You can't solve your problems by running away. I demand that you renounce this intention!

GISA: I'm sorry.

PAUL: Promise me. Now and forever.

GISA: I promise. I do.

PAUL and GISA float together, holding each other.

> ADRIANA: *Speaking across time as she sits in the Munich Station.*
> I promise, I do.
> I promise.
> I do.
>
> Remember: there is always some good.
>
> She came into the box of walls
> that formed the cell
> A young woman,
> under guard herself,
> watched as she watches.
>
> A dry piece of bread.
> Something black called coffee.
> Evening, a bowl of soup.
> She came into the cell.

Silence Not A Love Story

She did her deeds, efficient, lean.

The walls give no response.
To reverie; to rage; to silence itself.
She came into the cell.
Silently, unseen, formed words.
'Chin.' 'Up.'

She came into the cell.
She did her deeds.
Inside the empty walls.
Remember, said her lips,
There is some good.

Scene 9: Hamburg, On the Streets and At a Cemetery, 1933-36.

In a series of crossovers, GISA, PAUL, FRANZ and other people — SS, Brown Shirts, police — walk along. GISA hands out newsletters, pulling them from under a sleeve. The scene as a whole marks a passage of 3 years' time.

Subscene a

GISA: *She cautiously stops passersby.* Information you should have.

A WOMAN nods, takes sheet; another does not. FRANZ swings by, doesn't look at GISA.

FRANZ: A schoolteacher who lost her job is opening a bookstall. She only has a little money to pay.

GISA: A little is better than what I have.

FRANZ writes down an address, puts it under a bench. HIS goal is not to hide the paper so much as to keep people from connecting him and GISA.

FRANZ: I'll pass on your name.

GISA sits on the bench. Waits for a police officer to pass, picks up the address, exits.

Subscene b

Months later, PAUL and FRANZ stand on opposite sides of an advertising column, back to back.

PAUL: Two of our people were questioned.

FRANZ: They'll be pressed for descriptions. We need to increase security measures.

PAUL: I'll get out my tools.

Subscene c

Weeks later, PAUL and GISA stand in the cemetery. PAUL hands GISA a lunchbox — a small pail with a lid.

PAUL: You must eat.

GISA: I haven't time.

PAUL: Open it.

GISA opens the pail and pulls out a roll.

GISA: Kind of you.

PAUL: There's more.

GISA pulls out a piece of paper.

GISA: "Her home lies on the sea of freedom on which my boat sails and finds itself mirrored."

Henrik Ibsen. I'll cherish it.

PAUL: There's more.

GISA feels the pail, finds nothing. PAUL points and motions, as if a charade, that she should pull up the bottom. SHE tries and finally seeing a false bottom, laughs.

GISA: Beautiful. Your hands are beautiful.

Silence Not A Love Story   79

FRANZ enters and puts flowers on a gravestone. GISA hands him the lunch pail. FRANZ looks, slaps PAUL on the back.

FRANZ: Nice.

Scene 10: Hamburg, In a Park, 1936.

GISA walks, outdoors, alone, in a park by a river. She speaks to herself. The time is 1936.

GISA: So let me understand for myself. Did we forget something? 'April 1933: 'Playwright Bertolt Brecht is in exile.' 'SS enforces a boycott of Jewish businesses.' 'Nazis occupy trade union houses.' 'SS riots attack Jehovah's Witnesses.' 'Ten thousand homosexuals arrested.'

PAUL enters, hauling an object. HE circles GISA and then walks up to her, face to face.

PAUL: How fortunate that we're both enjoying the same sunshine in the same way. *HE whispers.* I checked: no one is near! Let's keep walking and talking: friends meeting for a stroll. I have a new invention to show you.

GISA: Did you hear the radio today? Quoting an American by the name of Brundage — Avery Brundage. From the U.S. Olympics. "I'm very glad to have visited Mr. Himmler. I can tell you, from my meetings in Berlin: the Jews are content."

> ADRIANA: *Speaking across time from the Munich Station.*
> When? When?
> When?

GISA looks to ADRIANA, but turns back, saying nothing.

GISA: "There's no reason why the U.S. should decline to participate in the Olympics in Berlin."

So I'm asking myself: why doesn't he know?

PAUL: He wants sports, he doesn't care about the rest. But my invention will cheer you!

GISA: How can he avoid the truth?

PAUL: Remember the lunch bucket I rigged?

GISA: Of course. You open it: "Look, a bread roll." (*Mimes.*) But flip up a secret flap and below is a false compartment that holds our newsletters. And at this moment, I'm reviewing every "Spark" headline from the past three years since 1933 so I may be able to understand this Mr. Brundage.

PAUL: There's nothing to understand.

I have something even better than the lunch bucket! For the Olympics!

> ADRIANA:
> We are in 1936, then?
> Is that what you are saying?

> GISA:
> Yes, right, right.

> ADRIANA:
> 1936.
> Two years ago.
> 1936.

GISA: I'm trying to identify: in what ways did we fail to get the point across?

PAUL: You simply can't reach everyone. Can I show you? — our time for a stroll is short!

GISA: This is important. 'May 1933: Tens of thousands of books are declared 'unGerman' and burned in a public fires.' You remember that one?

PAUL: Of course.

GISA: The next month, June 1933. 'Hitler regulates all newspapers.' 'Elderly Jewish man forced to parade with a sign: 'I am a Jew, but I support the Nazis.'' 'Sterilization is authorized of persons deemed 'unfit.''

PAUL: That's plenty. If you will allow me to show you this, I think it'll improve your mood.

HE holds up a piece of luggage.

GISA: I'm not finished.

PAUL: Please take a look!

GISA looks.

GISA: It's a piece of luggage.

PAUL: When you're determined, nothing will stop you.

       ADRIANA:
  Nothing will stop you.

GISA: 'September 1933: Jews banned from art, farming and theater.' 'April 1934: 'New courts are established to handle 'enemies' of the state.' 'June 1934: Hitler murders former ally Ernest Rohm, calling him a homosexual and traitor. Germans express approval at Hitler's decisiveness.'

PAUL: Gisa... this isn't necessary.

GISA: We report event after event, one after another — horizontally. Individually, each can be overlooked. But pile them on top of each other and they become mountains of evidence that no civilized person can ignore. Not even Avery Brundage. 'November 1935: Jews are disqualified from German citizenship.' '1936: Hitler plans an elaborate Olympics display.' And, three years after he disappeared, I still don't know what happened to my friend Rudy!

PAUL: You skipped one. 'September 15, 1935.'

GISA: I don't care to mention it.

PAUL: 'Germany issues the Law for the Protection of German Blood and Honor: non-Jews are prohibited from marrying Jews.' We should've married when we had a chance. But then your father wouldn't have approved.

GISA: I think he had a change of heart before he died.

PAUL: What does it say for you to avoid even mentioning September 15?

GISA: Very well, if you insist. 'September 15, 1935. Germany passes Nuremberg Laws: Mixed Jewish and Aryan marriages prohibited.' Are you satisfied?

PAUL: You're mocking me.

GISA: Of course not. We feel the same about one another whether or not we're married.

PAUL: Except my feelings are illegal: I'm 'too Aryan' for you. How do you think that makes me feel?

GISA: But why can't Avery Brundage see what's happening?

PAUL: This is my invention. People will be coming to Germany for the Olympics from all over. Franz and I will walk with them, carrying our luggage, every bit the spectator. *HE demonstrates with his luggage.* 'But, oh, I'm tired and must put down my bag.'

HE feigns being tired, puts the luggage down. GISA watches.

GISA: Yes?

PAUL: Keep watching.

HE picks his luggage up and points to the ground.

See!

GISA: There's an imprint on the ground where your luggage sat! From some mechanism inside?

PAUL: Exactly.

GISA: *SHE leans to the ground, reading.*

'All... is... not... well. Germany's calm... is the calm... of a... graveyard.'

PAUL: But while you read, I'm walking away.

GISA: Mr. Konopka: I think Avery Brundage has met his match.

Scene 11: Munich Train Station, 1938.

>ADRIANA:
>Her hands put coffee on the table.
>The guard watches from the door.
>Her eyes look at me,
>shift up.
>Her eyes shift up.
>No words. A shift. Up.
>
>Eventually, I lift the cup.
>A gift.
>A gift only someone who has been
>inside the cell can understand.
>The gift of a needle.
>The gift of a purpose.
>The gift of my hands.
>Shift.
>Up.

Scene 12: Hamburg, On the Streets, 1936.

GISA buttons a coat, leaving a bookshop where she works. HILDE rushes up, her face covered by a scarf.

HILDE: Hello! *Then whispering.* Gisa!

GISA: You're mistaken. I don't know you.

HILDE: I need to tell you something.

> ADRIANA:
> When?

> GISA:
> The year of the Olympics.

GISA: *Speaking to HILDE, she turns her back and deliberately speaks on a different subject.*

I'm sorry. I don't know that address.

HILDE: I took soup to Paul's apartment for his mother. They're waiting for him.

GISA: *Deliberately evasive.* I'm not very good with directions, I'm afraid.

HILDE: *Whispers.* Gestapo.

GISA: But perhaps a delivery truck can point you in the right direction.

HILDE: They wanted to know where he was during the Olympics.

GISA: Or perhaps a map from the bookstall will help. It's there. I do hope you find your way.

HILDE scoots away. GISA moves quickly and with determination.

> ADRIANA:
> One skin is made of leather.
> The other is made of steel.

Scene 13: Hamburg, In a Park, 1936.

PAUL, on his usual path, walks by GISA. He carries laundry and walks his bicycle. SHE steps with him.

GISA: Don't.

> ADRIANA:
> Don't.
> Don't smile.
> Don't laugh.
> Don't cry.
> Don't.

PAUL: I'm only carrying my laundry home.

GISA: Don't. Don't go. Don't walk. Don't return.

PAUL: What are you saying?

GISA: Ride. Into the woods. Into the country. Into the distance. Up to Blankensee.

I'll meet you there in two days. *SHE pauses momentarily.* Your apartment is compromised.

Scene 14. Outside Hamburg, 1936.

GISA and PAUL lie in the woods in dim light.

PAUL: Touch my face. So I can memorize how it feels.

GISA does.

GISA: I've tucked a poem in your jacket. They say once you get to Holland, the underground will get you to Paris.

PAUL: I'll ride to the border in two days, I think. A single one, if it isn't rainy. I could even carry a passenger on my bike.

GISA: There's much more work to do here.

PAUL: I could stay.

GISA: Don't be a fool.

PAUL: Now I'm a fool?

GISA: You'll be arrested and who knows what will happen next. No one will benefit.

PAUL: Come with me.

GISA: The committee collected the documents for you. I have Franz.

PAUL, standing, gets dressed.

PAUL: And they didn't tell you that no one has seen Franz for a week?

GISA: That can't be.

PAUL: *Seeing her distress.* You must remember, Gisa, there is always some good.

PAUL reaches down, kisses her and begins to exit. Before SHE can react fully, HE returns abruptly. Newsletter... I need to take one ,,,.

GISA: No. I'm not giving it to you.

PAUL: So you wish to argue with me? Now?

GISA: It's too dangerous to carry anti-Nazi literature.

PAUL: Europe is obsessing about a playboy king in Britain and the 'tragedy' of his giving up the throne to marry an American divorcee? While our lives are torn apart and our newsletter reports that Nazi factories are making poison gas and this is our last goodbye. If I want a newsletter to tell the world, don't you think that's for me to decide?

GISA finds the newsletters rolled in a stocking and straps one inside the leg of PAUL's pants.

GISA: Be careful the bicycle chain doesn't catch your pants.

PAUL: *Hugging her.* Bon courage. That's from Rilke, isn't it?

GISA: Rilke — yes.

PAUL: Eat, Gisa. That's from me. Remember to eat.

PAUL leaves. GISA sits alone in the woods, and then doubles over, as if about to throw up.

GISA: God!

> ADRIANA:
> And when they grinned and spat
> and left us weeping
> and left us all alone, and left no love...,

GISA: They will not see me cry.

She stuffs newsletters in a tree hollow; others in her shirt.

> ADRIANA:
> You, who then must have seen us from above
> bear testimony, that we were not sleeping.
> If you are there at all, bear witness, God!

Scene 15: Munich Train Station, 1938.

ADRIANA sits at the Munich Station. A newsboy comes through, holding up newspapers and reading off the headlines.

> NEWSBOY: Germany Adds Seven Million Austrians! See photos:
> Newspaper, ma'am?

Approached by the Newsboy, ADRIANA shakes her head 'no.' The newsboy moves on.

> NEWSBOY:
> Anschluss! 'Fürher Declared 'Man of the Year.'

THE WOMAN from SCENE ONE taps NEWSBOY, but speaks to ADRIANA.

> THE WOMAN:
> I'll throw a penny to a piece of history! Why not?

The NEWSBOY gives her a paper.

Scene 16: Hamburg, In a Park, On the Streets, 1936.

GISA returns to the wooded area where she and Paul were last together, retrieving more newsletters. SHE walks along, placing them in every spot she can find — on theater posts, in doorways, on seemingly empty benches. AN SS OFFICER comes her way. GISA sits, as if getting sun. SS OFFICER sees a newsletter and picks it up and puts it in a notebook of evidence. GISA waits, then quickly leaves.

> ADRIANA:
> Dive.
> Dive deep.
> Dive.
> Bon courage.

Scene 17: Hamburg, Gisa's Room, 1936; Munich Train Station 1938.

GISA is asleep in her room. Darkness and quiet are slowly interrupted by growing sounds: voices, footsteps, a key. GISA, in a nightgown, sits up, moves some papers, swallows some items, returns to bed. The door to the room is opened. Lights come on abruptly. Two HAMBURG SS MEN stand with FRIEDA, who speaks in a rush of words.

FRIEDA: I'd tell you more. But I only rent the room. My husband was a soldier, killed, so naturally I need the money. She doesn't have any friends. Doesn't do anything but read and ride her bicycle.

Doesn't even eat.

HAMBURG SS MAN 1: Doesn't eat?

FRIEDA: Hardly.

HAMBURG SS MAN 1: No sausages?

FRIEDA: Never. No sausages. No wurst. No eel.

HAMBURG SS MAN 1 bangs the floor, throws back Gisa's covers. HAMBURG SS MAN 2 starts throwing papers everywhere, searching.

HAMBURG SS MAN 1: Get up!

GISA sits, while HE speaks to FRIEDA. Thank you, ma'am. You may leave now.

FRIEDA exits. SS MAN speaks to GISA, and then he grabs her and stands her up.

Get dressed. I SAID: Get dressed.

GISA is frozen. HAMBURG SS MAN 1 pulls off GISA's nightgown. GISA stands, naked. HAMBURG SS MAN 1 stares. GISA finds some clothes, and begins to put them on. When SHE starts to turn her back, HE swivels her around.

HAMBURG SS MAN 2 finds GISA's Kollwitz prints, shows them to HAMBURG SS MAN 1, tosses them back.

HAMBURG SS MAN 2: Garbage.

HAMBURG SS MAN 1: She's a Jew.

HAMBURG SS MAN 2: Did she think she could hide it?

HAMBURG SS MAN 1: *To GISA.* Pig.

HAMBURG SS MAN 2: She'll have plenty of names to give.

HAMBURG SS MAN 2 exits.

> ADRIANA: *In simultaneous action, at the MUNICH station.*
> Remember
> To forget.
> Pretend.
> Lie if you must.
> Remember
> To forget.

In simultaneous action to HAMBURG, TWO MUNICH SS MEN approach and stand over ADRIANA. One holds out a hand, seeking papers, while the other watches. ADRIANA hands up a passport to MUNICH SS MAN 1, who scrutinizes it.

> MUNICH SS MAN 2: A Jew?

> MUNICH SS MAN 1: No. French father, Austrian mother.

HE passes the papers back to ADRIANA; THEY walk off.

HAMBURG SS MAN 2 returns to GISA's room, towing HILDE, whose hands are tied in front of her. HILDE is crying. SS MAN 2 speaks to HILDE, pointing at GISA.

HAMBURG SS MAN 2: Know this one?

HILDE: I HAVE THREE BROTHERS AND A SISTER TO CARE FOR! PLEASE!

HAMBURG SS MAN 2: We'll put them in the wagon together.

HAMBURG SS MAN 1 ties GISA's hands.

HAMBURG SS MAN 1: Oink.

HAMBURG SS MAN 1 suddenly spits at GISA. HILDE watches. SS I ties their hands together, marches them out.

> ADRIANA:
> We go, we go,
> the difficult steep and long way.
> In us lives a will, good and clear
> We do not cry any more.

Scene 18: Fuhlsbüttel, Outside Hamburg, 1936.

GISA sits in a plain brown dress. GESTAPO MAN enters. The GESTAPO MAN lights up a cigarette, offers one to GISA.

GESTAPO MAN: Cigarette? *GISA declines with a gesture.* Don't smoke? *GISA says nothing.*

I hear some anti-patriot groups tell their members to stop smoking so they won't be tempted by our offers of cigarettes. True?

GISA: I don't know.

GESTAPO MAN: I see. It was a bit of humor. We just need the answers to a few questions.

GISA says nothing.

> ADRIANA: *Across time.* Where are you?
>
> GISA: I don't know.
>
> ADRIANA: Oh.
> Bon courage. Bon courage.
> Bon courage.
> Keep your wits about you.
> Remember to forget.

GESTAPO MAN: Who wrote this newsletter?

GISA: I never saw it before.

GESTAPO MAN: Who wrote the article that claims the Führer is making poison gas in Hamburg? Nicely written.

GISA: I don't know anything about it.

GESTAPO MAN: What do you know about poison gas?

GISA: I don't know anything about it.

GESTAPO MAN: Who are your closest friends?

GISA: I stick to myself.

GESTAPO MAN: How old are you?

GISA: Twenty-six.

GESTAPO MAN: You're young to be so friendless. Who is Willie Eichler?

GISA: I don't know.

GESTAPO MAN: Did he leave the Homeland so an innocent girl could hold the bag for him?

GISA: I'm not aware of the situation you're describing.

GESTAPO MAN: Who is Franz Haberman?

GISA: I don't know.

GESTAPO MAN: Used to work for a printer in Hamburg? He's your friend, isn't he?

GISA: No.

GESTAPO MAN: Odd. He remembers you as a friend. Remembered you.

    ADRIANA:
    Remember the traps.
    Remember the lies.
    Remember to keep your wits.

GISA: I don't know him.

GESTAPO MAN: Who is Hilde Hoch?

GISA: I don't know.

GESTAPO MAN: Who is Gerhardt Konopka?

GISA: I don't know.

GESTAPO MAN: Paul Konopka, perhaps, to you?

> ADRIANA:
> Remember this also when you grow old.
> Remember there is art, there is poetry.
> Remember a skin of leather and steel.
> Remember to grow old.

GISA: It's not a name I'm familiar with.

GESTAPO MAN: Have you ever worked for a labor union?

GISA: No.

GESTAPO MAN: Did you pass out labor 'newsletters' at the ElbeTunnel?

GISA: No.

GESTAPO MAN: Did you ever try to unionize a factory?

GISA: No.

GESTAPO MAN: Did you meet often with other members of the ISK?

GISA: I don't know what it is.

GESTAPO MAN: *HE puts his face into hers.* You should learn to smoke.

HE blows smoke at her. You're a nasty traitor. A stubborn streak. But we have time. Perhaps your memory will improve in solitary. This is a thousand year Reich. I'll ask the guards to leave a knife on the table, so you can spare us the trouble.

ADRIANA: *Across time, furious.*
You can't let him say that!
Say something back!
Say, you're a hateful bastard!
Say, I know all about your terror tactics!
Say. I'm not going to give into your lies and deceits!
Spit. SPIT NOW.

GISA: *Pointedly ignoring ADRIANA, speaking with studied calm.* I've told you all that I know.

GESTAPO MAN: Now that I think about it, solitary can wait. First, perhaps, you will enjoy the box. Guards! This prisoner wishes to stand in the box. And don't bother with dinner — it's too late for all that.

HE blows smoke in the air and exits. TWO WORKERS enter, put GISA in a standing coffin. THEY exit, leaving darkness.

ADRIANA: *Across time.*
Use your imagination.
Remember song.

GISA:
I hate THEM. I HATE them. I HATE them.

ADRIANA:
Remember art.
Remember poetry.
Remember Rilke.

"When dogs are sleeping, and when stones are lying
Woe, a sad night, woe, just any night
which waits until the morning should return...."

GISA:
"...until the morning should return.
For angels do not come to such in prayer

and nights do not become great for their sake."

    ADRIANA:
Dive deep.
Swim.
Swim the Alster. Swim the Elbe.
Dive.

Scene 19: Fuhlsbüttel, Outside Hamburg, 1936.

The next morning. LIGHTS come up. An OLD MAN, a guard but not dressed in an SS uniform, opens the box, a standing coffin. GISA practically falls out.

OLD MAN: My goodness, young woman, here, stand, lean on me. *GISA does.*

There, there. These crazy men from Munich. It's criminal. How long have you been in there?

GISA: I don't know.

OLD MAN: Do you know where you are?

GISA: No.

    ADRIANA:
    Where? Where?

OLD MAN: Our fine old Hamburg prison, look what they've done to it.

    ADRIANA:
    Fuhlsbüttel.
    There are so many rumors about Fuhlsbüttel.
    People go in; people don't come out.

OLD MAN: They've turned our fine old Fuhlsbüttel prison into a chamber of horrors. We've run the prison very well for 60 years without them. Look at these boxes... coffins. Who thought that up? Some lunatic, that's who. Do you know your name?

GISA: Gisa Peiper.

OLD MAN: Then you haven't lost your senses. Not like the one screaming in the night: 'Let me out. Yes, I did listen to the French radio. Let me go!'

GISA is woozy. SHE turns and sees a knife on a table and picks it up.

GISA: They left a knife for me.

OLD MAN: *HE tries to pry the knife from her hands.* No, no. I'll take that. Hand it to me. I have a better place for that.

Have you eaten?

GISA: Eaten?

OLD MAN: You must eat. Now, you give me this knife, and I'll get you some hot soup. And none of their grovel. Soup my wife packed for lunch.

HE takes the knife, and puts it in his boot.

GISA: You look like an angel.

OLD MAN: Now, don't say things like that or I'll think you've lost your mind. Like the Jehovah's Witness girl. *HE whispers.* They broke both her hands because she won't swear allegiance. You remember who you are.

GISA: Thank you.

Scene 20: Fuhlsbüttel, Outside Hamburg, 1936.

GISA is in a cell. SHE marches three steps forward, turns, three steps back.

GISA: Today I am walking the path to Blankensee. That takes two hours. Three steps forward, three steps back, keep the mind alive.

Let's see now, if one walks six steps in three seconds, that would be 120 steps in a minute, and 7,200 steps an hour; 3,600 times back and forth in the cell. Imagination will keep me alive.

Singing.

"Who wants to hike in joy

Must rise early, meeting the sun..."

Keep busy. But what to do with the hands? And with the eyes? And ears?

> ADRIANA: *Speaking across time.*
> Don't look. Don't look out the window.
> Don't see who is barking orders. Don't see who is wincing.
> Do not see with your own eyes
> the images that will not
> go away.
> Don't look.

As ADRIANA talks, GISA climbs on a chair and looks out the bars of a window. Looking out, SHE rubs her hands rapidly on her dress.

GISA: Who are the men who do this? Yelling 'roll over?' And who are you... forced on all fours? What thing of courage did you do? To bring you here? Quietly, to herself. You, out the window, this is from me to you. 'I see the blood fill your mouth, I see red pour from your nose, I see you stumble and fall.' YOU have renewed my fury and fury will keep me alive.

GISA returns to walking, furiously, stretching her hands open and closed.

> ADRIANA:
> This is a poem
> Not a prayer.
> This is a promise
> Not a song.

> Your last hot breath sears the air,
> burnishes steel beneath my gown.
> I am your witness
> And this is not a prayer.

The cell door opens at the prison. A PRISON TRUSTEE, a woman, brings a cup of coffee, and looks all around. THE TRUSTEE mouths words to GISA and points to the bottom of the cup, and then to a place on the wall. SHE exits.

> ADRIANA:
> Chin.
> Up.
> Chin up. Chin up.

GISA walks to the place on the wall where the trustee had pointed, and running her hand over it, finds words scratched into the stone.

GISA: 'You who come after us, do not despair. The sun will also shine for us.'

GISA looks under the cup. SHE finds a needle, and walks back to the wall and scratches into it.

'For, amid darkness, angels still dwell; it is for each of us, each day to decide.'

GISA finds a thread in the hem of her dress, unravels it, and threads the needle.

Scene 21: Munich Train Station, 1938; Fuhlsbüttel, Outside Hamburg, 1937.

> ANNOUNCER: *Loud speaker, Munich Station.* In 30 minutes, the train for Paris will arrive on track eight. Passengers, have your documents ready for inspection.

ADRIANA straightens herself, but doesn't move.

GISA is in the Fuhlsbüttel prison. The time is early in 1937. In a lapse of three months, her sewing project is more extensive and she hides it under her dress as the door opens. A young SS Guard enters. GISA stands.

YOUNG SS GUARD: Ready for questioning?

GISA: If you wish.

YOUNG SS GUARD: A cooperative one! *HE laughs.* And we don't even need you anymore: these three months have given us everything we want. We know all about you and your 'leaders.'

GISA: I see.

The GUARD pushes up against GISA with his body.

YOUNG SS GUARD: They said I can let you go. We're running short of space. What do you think? You want to go? Just you and me here and it's been a long night of cold air in Fuhlsbüttel.

> ADRIANA:
> Don't be tricked.
> Every minute could bring a trick.
> Keep your wits about you.

GISA slides out from under him.

GISA: Of course you must know I'm not as young as you might think.

YOUNG SS GUARD: You don't think I'd touch a traitor, do you?

Answer! You didn't answer.

GISA: All of the guards have been true to their oath.

YOUNG SS GUARD: Just know — once you leave, we'll be following you everywhere. Nothing escapes us. You are hereby ordered not tell anyone what happened to you or anything that you've seen. Understood?

GISA *nods.*

Because you can be invited for a return visit. I'll keep my eye out!

THE GUARD *laughs. HE menaces as if he's going to grab GISA sexually, but pushes HER in front instead. THEY exit.*

    ADRIANA:
    And when they grinned and spat
    And left us weeping
    And left us all alone, and left no love,
    You, who then must have seen us from above
    Bear testimony, we were not sleeping.

Scene 22: Hamburg, On the Streets, 1937; Munich Train Station, 1938.

GISA stands outside the prison, in street clothes. SHE shivers and trembles.

    ADRIANA:
    Don't look back.

GISA looks up, listens, and runs.

    ADRIANA:
    Don't smile.
    Don't stop.
    Don't laugh.
    Don't cry.

GISA: *To ADRIANA.* HOW can you tell me not to cry!

GISA stops, pulls out the cloth handkerchief stuffed in her dress. SHE clings to it and fingers its corners. Look at this stitching. My sanity, in every plunge of the needle!

HILDE: *Aged, SHE calls, also exiting prison.* Gisa! Wait. Gisa! Gisa... my leg... I can't run.

GISA clutches the handkerchief, and runs in the opposite direction.

In the Munich Train Station, THE WOMAN from the first scene brushes by ADRIANA and taps her on the knee.

> THE WOMAN:
> The Paris train is coming, honey.

ADRIANA looks up, confused, says nothing.

> THE WOMAN:
> You're waiting for the Paris train, aren't you? It won't be long.

Speaking now as if GISA might be deaf.

> You're going to need to get to the platform.

SHE points.

> The train won't stop for you here, and it won't stop long before it's gone again.

ADRIANA takes out a handkerchief, coughs, nods as if to say she understands and 'thank you.' THE WOMAN moves on.

Scene 23: Hamburg, Berlin, Karlsbad, Various sites, 1937; Munich Train Station, 1938.

GISA, breathless, running, enters the cemetery. SHE falls down, clutching herself. A VOICE calls - it is FRANZ, not visible at first.

FRANZ: We meet again.

GISA: *Hears the voice and quickly grasps who the speaker is.* You're alive!

FRANZ *steps out. He speaks lightly, with humor, although he limps, his face is bandaged and arm mangled.*

FRANZ: Half-alive. Parts of me are alive.

GISA: My God! What have they done!

FRANZ: Doesn't hurt much anymore. Except when I'm awake. Or when I'm asleep.

GISA: Fuhlsbüttel?

FRANZ: Jailhouse, back of a wagon: they can always find a place. And a person. Which, I guess, was — me! My family found a boat. Thankfully.

GISA: I embroidered the corners of a cloth pulled from my dress. Recited poetry. Sang camp songs. And the things I saw out the window...

Who did this to us? Who turned us in?

>   ADRIANA:
>   Don't.
>   Don't think.
>   Don't dwell.

FRANZ: Don't, Gisa. You can hear boats ripple along the Elbe — that's enough.

GISA: They've burned scars into my memory. At any moment, they could re-arrest us. My legs — they're trembling, like they're not even a part of my body. Next time, I won't come out alive. Truth is, some days, I didn't want to come out alive. I stayed alive to spite them.

FRANZ: One thing I know about you, Gisa Peiper — you have a stubborn streak!

HE pauses a moment.

But now, we need to make plans to get you to safety.

GISA: And you, too.

FRANZ: And not 'me, too.' Of course, we're both bait. No one can take a chance on being seen with us. But I'm a heavy piece of luggage. Can't be inconspicuous. Can't be conspicuous. Things are different for you.

GISA: They stamped my passport: 'stateless.' Closes all the doors. If I leave illegally, it'll mean trouble for everyone. I've seen how they harass Paul's mother. 'Your son didn't send you a message, Mrs. Konopka?' My mother won't budge from Berlin, even though my sister sent her papers for Palestine.

FRANZ: I see that there's one deed left for me. I'll get word to the underground that you're alive and where you'll be. And here's what you must do:

As FRANZ talks, GISA rises and begins doing the things HE describes. FRANZ edges himself off stage, still talking; OTHERS come and go, as indicated by FRANZ.

Go back to your room, quietly gather your things. Take only the essentials. Act as if you're going on an overnight stay. When your landlady inquires, say nothing.

GISA gathers her things. SHE changes clothes. SHE picks up and puts back her Kollwitz prints; then picks them up and packs them. FRIEDA enters and gesticulates, points, throws her hands up, but GISA quietly keeps packing.

FRANZ: Go straightaway to Berlin. Pack your mother up to be resettled. You must tell her you're a freedom fighter, and the Gestapo shows no mercy. Board her on a boat.

GISA enters her mother's home, finds her MOTHER, sitting alone. GISA sweeps the room; fixes her mother's hair, puts a coat on her. GISA sticks the handkerchief from the prison in her mother's pocket, kisses her.

FRANZ: Next, find a doctor at the Czechoslovakian Embassy. White hair. Slender build. Round glasses. Tell him you need to go to Karlsbad Springs immediately for health reasons. A "stateless" person can leave for medical care. Say that you're feeling very tired. Severe arthritis. And your kidneys bother you. He'll write a note that says you need to travel to Czechoslovakia for treatment.

GISA: *From a distant place, speaks to FRANZ.* Inside the Czech embassy, there's a man who helps the resistance?

GISA enters a doctor's office, lies on exam table. The DOCTOR says nothing to her. GISA coughs, points . The DOCTOR takes out a pad, and writes quickly.

FRANZ: Underground workers will meet you in Karlsbad. Wear white gloves so that they may identify you. They'll relocate you to a country where you can be useful. They'll have a key word - ISK - and the person meeting you will use Morse code to tap it in your hand. They'll find an Austrian citizen to marry you. Or a Dane.

GISA carefully puts on gloves. SHE carries her bags. An UNDERGROUND WORKER approaches and, with a two-handed shake to her one hand, taps a message into her palm. GISA acknowledges it. The UNDERGROUND WORKER introduces an older Austrian man, MR. KUEHN, who nods.

FRANZ: As a spouse, you'll be allowed to travel to your husband's native land.

GISA: *Speaking across time to FRANZ.* What about Paul? He'll be devastated.

FRANZ: This is an anti-Nazi movement, Gisa. This isn't about Paul.

GISA: But...

FRANZ: We swore to put the movement first. We made a COMMITMENT.

ADRIANA: *From the Munich station.*
You should be with me and so softly
Touch me as a good, far away dream.
I want to lie near you - oh, so quietly...
your arm should be around me
and all this that the day demands
should sink away, and rest.

GISA turns to the UNDERGROUND WORKER.

GISA: I realize you have the best of intentions. But I should have made it plain that I have someone already. In Paris. Part of the movement. I'll be joining him — I can't marry.

UNDERGROUND WORKER: *Pointedly ignores her.* The ceremony shall be at a lawyer's office this afternoon. None of this was easy to arrange, but the instructions came from Willie Eichler and Minna Specht. They said you're a good, hard worker, one to be trusted. We need good workers in Austria.

ADRIANA: *Across time, she speaks to GISA.* When? When is this?

GISA: *Turning to ADRIANA from her conversation with the WORKER.*
You know the answer.

ADRIANA: I need to hear it.

GISA:
Last year. 1937.

ADRIANA:
One year ago?

GISA:
One year — is long enough.

UNDERGROUND WORKER: After the ceremony, we shall give you new papers. You shall take the name of Mr. Kuehn. Your first name shall be Adriana. Remember it. French father, Austrian mother. You must forget otherwise who you are, forget your name, forget your father, forget your mother, forget your past, forget the someone in Paris. Together, you and your new husband shall travel to Vienna, where the movement is working to stop the Nazi spread.

ADRIANA, in the MUNICH station, looks at a clock, checks her ticket, stands, collects items around her and begins to move away from the bench on which she has been sitting.

GISA: They'll detect my accent. Prussian German is very different from Austrian German. I could be a danger to everyone, including Mr. Kuehn.

UNDERGROUND WORKER: This is true. All of us could end up in prison! Or dead. Probably will. That doesn't mean we shall be silenced!

GISA: Austria could be overtaken within a year. The Nazis are on the move...

UNDERGROUND WORKER: All the more reason to put our best people there. If Austria becomes unsafe, we shall move the workers to Paris. *Pauses.* If you're uncertain, or ambivalent, tell me now.

GISA: I can't swear allegiance to Mr. Kuehn. I can't pretend. It would be a lie.

UNDERGROUND WORKER: Don't be foolish, and especially don't be a foolish romantic. Gather your courage, my dear. Our movement is a thin reed standing up to big lies. Of course, there are dangers —

GISA: You don't have to lecture me. I KNOW THE DANGERS! I've been a witness to the dangers!

UNDERGROUND WORKER: Very well, then; there's nothing more to say.

GISA: *Now, to Mr. KUEHN.* Mr. Kuehn, understand that I will be a wife in name only. *She pauses.* Love is... a stubborn streak.

MR. KUEHN, *somewhat baffled, nods.*

ADRIANA *begins to move from her perch at the station to train platform at the Munich station.*

> ADRIANA:
> Behind us lies the burden of long years
> behind us all the sorrow we have suffered...
>
> When wild the wind blows over darkened fields
> We only feel the clear wide space.
> When darkened clouds press full of threat
> In us now grows a calm, strong as a tree.

GISA *looks over to* ADRIANA.

UNDERGROUND WORKER: Now give me these and follow.

The UNDERGROUND WORKER *reaches for* GISA's *things.* GISA *grabs her bag and struggles for control of it.*

GISA: I'll carry these. Art prints. Käthe Kollwitz. Perfect for a newlywed in Austria.

THE UNDERGROUND WORKER *yanks away the prints.*

UNDERGROUND WORKER: Then we shall find a lovely home for them, Adriana. The past... is past.

THE UNDERGROUND WORKER *takes packages, exits.* KUEHN *holds out his arm, but when* GISA *doesn't take it,* HE *exits with the* WORKER. GISA *stands, holding herself, arms wrapped around her body.*

FRANZ: *Only his voice is heard.* We'll get word to Paul. He'll want to know that you're safe.

ADRIANA:
One skin of leather.
the other of steel
Bon courage.

Scene 24: Munich Train Station, 1938.

At the Munich station, ADRIANA walks toward the platform, fingering her ticket, visa, other papers. GISA speaks to ADRIANA from an unspecific location, near where ADRIANA had been sitting at the Munich station.

GISA:

There is the goal —
yet one hesitates.
So far the way
And everywhere are stones.
Behind us lies the burden of long years
behind us all the sorrow we have suffered.

ADRIANA:
Why am I in Munich? Of all places, Munich!
Who agreed to return me to Germany?

GISA: *(Calmly, to ADRIANA.)*

Dive deep.
Swim.
Don't.
Don't laugh.
Don't smile.
Don't cry.
Don't.

ADRIANA:
No! Tell me! I want to know. The escape was a year ago!

You said so. The Czech doctor, the Karlsbad meeting, the underground, Mr. Kuehn. Why the Munich station, with the SS crawling in every corner?

GISA: Bon courage.

ADRIANA:
No! TELL ME WHY!

GISA: Tell you? What, Adriana? WHAT! Didn't you say the Nazi advance was on? Didn't you spend the year aiding resistance in Austria? A country, like a person, must have courage! Austria did not. What more is there, Adriana!

ADRIANA:
But Munich...?

GISA:

Hold on.
Please.
It's only one layover.
To Paris.
The worker told you.
Out of Austria, through Munich,
then the train to Paris.
The worker told you.
Please.

ADRIANA:
They left a knife on the table:
'Why not save us the trouble?'

GISA:

Don't think.

Dive deep.
Dive. Dive deep.

SOLDIER 1 in the Munich Station, calls out as ADRIANA approaches his area.

> SOLDIER 1: Before you step to the platform for the Munich train to Paris, line up to the right. Have your passport and identification open.

THE WOMAN handing around steins in the first scene lingers nearby the platform at the Munich station, hanging from time to time on the arm of SOLDIER 1. SOLDIER 1 takes ADRIANA's identification.

GISA: *To ADRIANA.*
One skin of leather, the other of steel. Underneath, a stubborn streak.

SOLDIER 1 shows ADRIANA's papers to SOLDIER 2. THEY scrutinize the documents.

> SOLDIER 1: *To ADRIANA.* Tell me your place of birth; your mother; your father.

ADRIANA coughs into a handkerchief, points to her throat.

> SOLDIER 1: Speak! I want to HEAR your voice! I want to HEAR your accent.
> I can't let you on the Paris train until I hear: place of birth, mother, father. Say, 'My mother is... My father is...'
> Do YOU WANT TO GET ON THE TRAIN OR NOT!

ADRIANA speaks to SOLDIER 1, for the first time saying words that are not part of an inner monologue.

> ADRIANA: My mother...

THE WOMAN suddenly cuts off ADRIANA, and speaks to SOLDER 1. SHE seems as if she might be drunk.

> THE WOMAN: It's Anschluss! You silly goose! I was just celebrating with her up in the waiting room. She's sick as a dog and still hoisting away in joy! I know everything there is to know about her, pet. Ask me.

THE WOMAN grabs ADRIANA's hand with both her hands for a moment. THE WOMAN quickly writes a code into ADRIANA'S hand. ADRIANA stands motionless, and seeing that THE WOMAN is wearing gloves, her mouth is frozen.

> THE WOMAN: Ask me the questions. What do you want to know!

THE WOMAN smacks a kiss on SOLDIER 1.

> THE WOMAN: Ask me, pet. Come on, ask me what we'll do tonight. It's Anschluss! Once in a lifetime.

> SOLDIER 1: *Laughs.* It's Anschluss! We'll celebrate, that's what.

As SOLDIER 1 kisses THE WOMAN, HE hands back the papers and waves ADRIANA through.

> SOLDIER 1: Spread the good news in Paris, eh?

ADRIANA nods, takes her papers, moves on.

GISA:
When will it start
the dawn of the day
when humanity

turns to the light
Yet it may be, whenever it will be.
I will work hard
as if the time has come today.
Remember...

    ADRIANA: Remember...

GISA:... Remember this also when you are old.

End of Play

Gisa Konopka – 1929, graduation from the "gymnasium." Courtesy Konopka Institute for Best Practices in Adolescent Health.

Outside Fuhlsbuttel. Gisa (Peiper) Konopka was imprisoned here in 1936. Courtesy Fuhlsbuttel Concentration Camp and Prison Memorial.

Inside Fuhlsbuttel Prison (prison cell) circa 1932. Courtesy Fuhlsbuttel Concentration Camp and Prison Memorial.

Labor demonstration, Germany 1930s.

Book burning, Germany 1930s.

German resisters prepare a leaflet.

Tools of resisters: A typewriter and a Gestetener.

Resistor in the woods.

Sculpture by Paul Konopka. Courtesy
Konopka Institute for Best Practices in
Adolescent Health.

Paul and Gisa 1929. Courtesy Konopka Institute for Best Practices in Adolescent Health.

At home on their porch 1970. Courtesy Konopka Institute for Best Practices in Adolescent Health.

Paul and Gisa. Courtesy Konopka Institute for Best Practices in Adolescent Health.

Willie Eichler and Minna Specht, leaders of the ISK (International Socialist Combat League).

Gisa Konopka at home, 2000. Courtesy Konopka Institute for Best Practices in Adolescent Health.
Photo by Richard G. Anderson

A Select and Abbreviated Chronology of the Time Period of the Play

1918—End of WWI; Gisa Peiper, age 8.

1919—The Versailles Treaty and formation of the Weimar Republic in Germany, a Parliamentary democracy to replace the Kaiser.

1919—WWI soldier Adolph Hitler attends German Workers' Party meeting in Munich.

1920—The German Workers' Party becomes the National Socialist German Workers' Party or NSDAP, later known as Nazis. The Austrian-born Hitler devotes himself to it. Other political parties also emerge in Germany's awkward new democracy.

1921—Hilter, considered a spellbinding speaker, takes over NSDAP.

1922—NSDAP organize Storm Troopers or Brown Shirts.

1923—Desperate inflation afflicts Germany.

1923—Hitler attempts to stage a political coup with ruffians in Munich.

1924—Hitler is tried for treason and convicted, but his views gain wide publicity.

1924—Imprisoned for 9 months, Hitler writes or dictates *Mein Kampf* (My Struggle). The Nazis opposed the Versailles treaty that limited German territory and powers. Nazis blamed the war's conclusion on Marxists, profiteers and international Jewry, which, along with the liberal political party of 'Social Democrats,' were declared responsible for inflation. The Nazi philosophy is one of hyper-nationalism, anti-semitism, anti-communism, a state-controlled economy, expansion of German territory, the unification of Aryan Germans into one "nation," and single-party dictatorship. In "*Mein Kampf*" Hitler declares that some "races" create civilization, others corrupt it. The best and most desirable, according to him, are Nordic-Aryan-Germans, whom he considers to be the "master race." The Jews were considered to be the enemy of all, and, he asserted, must be eliminated. Hitler gains support from prominent right-wing industrialists.

1925—The Nazi party, briefly banned, is re-launched by Hitler once released from prison

1926—The Nazis begin youth groups.

1927—A speaking ban on Hitler is lifted.

1927—Jewish cemeteries in Germany are desecrated.

1928—The Nazis win 2.6 percent of the vote, or 12 seats in Germany's Parliament, the Reichstag.

1929—Hitler appoints Henrich Himmler to head the SS; Gisa Peiper, age 19.

1929—Stock market crash in the US has worldwide implications.

1929—A Nazi rally in Nuremberg draws 100,000.

1930—3 million Germans, or 14 percent of the population, are jobless.

1930—In September, the Nazi party wins 18.3 percent of the vote and 109 seats in the Reichstag.

1931—A Munich paper writes about the Nazi plan to deprive Jews of citizenship.

1931—The German banks collapse.

1931—Jews in Berlin are attacked on their way to High Holy Day services.

1932—Hitler gets 11.3 percent of the vote in presidential election; while he campaigns for freedom and bread, Storm Troopers physically attack opposition.

1932—In a July vote, the Nazis get 37 percent and 230 seats in the Reichstag.

1932—The Nazis assume control in Dessau and begin repressive measures, evicting the modern Bauhaus design school.

1932—In a November election, the Nazis lose 34 seats in the Reichstag.

1932—Prominent Jews begin to leave, including Einstein.

1933—Jan 30. von Hindenburg, the German president, decides to appoint Hitler to the powerful position of Chancellor.

1933—Feb 2. Political demonstrations are banned.

1933—Feb 12. Communists are hunted down and killed.

1933—Feb 27. The Reichstag burns and a hapless Dutch Communist is blamed; civil liberties are suspended by Hitler and he assumes emergency powers. Historians believe the SS set the fire.

1933—Nazis open concentration camps.

1933—Mar 9. Nazi troopers stage riots against German Jews.

1933—Liberal German Social Democrats evacuate and set up in Prague.

1933—Apr 1. The government orders a boycott of all Jewish businesses.

1933—Apr 7. Non Aryan civil servants including teachers, are 'retired.'

1933—April. Playwright Bertolt Brecht is among those who leave Germany.

1933—June. Nazis occupy union houses and arrest labor leaders. Jehovah's Witnesses and homosexuals are arrested.

1933- New "race" laws institutionalizing anti-semitism are issued daily.

1933—May 10. 'UnGerman" books are burned in 30 towns.

1933—June. Hilter regulates all newspapers.

1933—July. Tens of thousands of Socialists and Communists are arrested.

1933—Sept. Jews are prohibited from theater, art, farming, professions. Sterilization is authorized of 'unfit' persons.

1933—Oct. Germany withdraws from the League of Nations.

1934—April. To handle 'enemies of the state' new courts are created with no juries and no appeal.

1934—June. Hitler murders former ally and SA leader Ernest Rohm, calling him a traitor and homosexual, and kills another 100 top SA officers allied with Rohm in the 'Night of Long Knives'; Germans approve his decisiveness.

1934—August. Hitler declares himself Führer and absolute leader.

1934—Sept. Hitler creates a secret air force.

1935—Sept 15. Jews are disqualified from German citizenship. Nuremberg laws are passed prohibiting intermarriage.

1936—Nazis begin producing poison gas.

1936—Olympics are held in Berlin; the US at first declines to attend, then agrees.

1938—March 14. Anschluss. Austria capitulates to Germany and in the "union" becomes a Germany-controlled territory; Gisa Peiper, age 28.

1938—Nov. 10. On Kristellnacht, the Night of Broken Glass, violent attacks are made on Jewish sites.

1939—Sept 1. World War II begins with the German invasion of Poland.

Postscript to *Silence Not A Love Story*

By Dr. Marilyn Frost

Silence Not A Love Story ends with Adriana saying, "Remember," and Gisa saying, "...remember this also when you are old." Gisela Peiper Konopka, the woman on whom the play is based, not only remembered until her death at ninety-three years of age in 2003, but also shared these stories throughout her long and remarkable life, along with a call to action. *Silence Not A Love Story* captures essences of Gisa. In the nine-year span of the story, we can see the seeds and themes of the enduring love and sense of overarching purpose that she and Paul shared, the importance of courage sustained by love, and the dignity and equality of all humans. The presence of Adriana throughout the play captures another essential aspect of Gisa's life: She experienced a lifelong inner tension, sometimes close to torment, between acknowledging what was wrong, while still finding the strength to try to create change.

Gisa wrote about her early life and years doing resistance work in Germany, Austria, Czechoslovakia, and France shortly after she arrived in the United States in 1941, but she did not publish her account until 1988 in a memoir, *Courage and Love* (Beaver's Pond Press). The late Janice Andrews-Schenk wrote a compelling biography published in 2006, *Rebellious Spirit: Gisela Konopka* (Beaver's Pond Press), that chronicles Gisa's life, her professional contributions to the theory and practice of social work and related fields, and her broader legacy as a humanitarian.

Silence Not A Love Story ends with Gisa boarding a train in Munich. In real life, the story continued in Paris, where she arrived from Munich and was reunited with an exhausted Paul. For more than two years Gisa and Paul continued their underground efforts, sometimes together and sometimes separated by prison, internment camps, and danger. Finally, they spent time in hiding, together in Southern France. For Gisa, even though this narrative is "an account of much horror, it is also one of LOVE!" Gisa shared stories of degradation and cruelty in *Courage and Love*; but there are also everyday heroes who showed small kindnesses, risked their own safety, or provided gestures of respect.

Gisa got her visa before Paul and even though neither wanted yet another uncertain separation, at Paul's insistence, Gisa made travel plans. To their unending joy, Paul was able to follow a few months later and they were married in New York City on June 23, 1941, after the mandatory three-day wait following Paul's arrival. Gisa loved to tell the story of their wedding. Gisa's "wedding dress" was the only good dress she owned, the "luxury" in which they indulged for the wedding consisted of deep blue bachelor buttons, and the honeymoon was a ride on the Staten Island Ferry. Gisa would also pause to remember that the terrors of the war were still real. But, above all, this event, after twelve years of not being able to wed, was a joy and the symbolic beginning of their life together in the United States, a place that Gisa and Paul loved deeply.

Gisa and Paul soon relocated to Pittsburgh, where Gisa became a graduate student in social work with an interest in group work at the University of Pittsburgh. Paul worked in a factory until he was drafted into the U.S. Army in 1942. Gisa had a field placement at the Pittsburgh Child Guidance Clinic and stayed on as a full-time group social worker after her graduation. This period provided the foundation for Gisa's professional career as an author, practitioner, teacher, and advocate. Gisa wanted to enrich and empower the lives of the children with whom she worked, as well as to influence other practitioners. Gisa began authoring professional publications, especially on children and social group work in 1944, and she published more than 300 articles and books over the next fifty years.

Gisa accepted a faculty position in the School of Social Work at the University of Minnesota in 1947. She and Paul moved to Minneapolis, Minnesota, a city and state they readily embraced. Gisa and Paul created lives of unrelenting hard work and meaningful contributions to others, and they flourished as individuals and together. Paul worked by day as an engineer at General Mills and, early on, spent the remainder of his time making a dilapidated cottage overlooking Lake Calhoun into a home. He later carved wood sculptures and created practical and decorative pieces that were proudly displayed.

Gisa would laugh when she recalled the places the snow would come in during their first winter. "It wasn't so warm and comfortable then!" This would be Gisa's home for more than fifty years and would remain so until she died, as she dearly desired. Their home became a temporary shelter for many over the years: a place for discussion, dialogue, and, in Gisa's words, "talking philosophy" with individuals of diverse ages and backgrounds, but with shared belief in the dignity of all. For Gisa, their home was a living symbol of what you could do with hard work and dedication, if given a chance.

Gisa's professional contributions to social work theory, research, practice, and education are many and well documented in *Rebellious Spirit*, Janice Schenk-Andrews' biography. Gisa received significant acknowledgement in her field, including designation as a founding Social Work Pioneer by the National Association of Social Workers.

In this area, Gisa is best known for her contributions to the development of social group work, which she defined in her classic text, *Social Group Work: A Helping Process* (Prentice-Hall 1963), as: "a method of social work which helps individuals to enhance their social functioning through purposeful group experiences and to cope more effectively with their personal, group or community problems."

Gisa saw social group work as an addition to casework and individual therapy in agencies such as child guidance clinics. She believed that the understanding of individuals needed to include understanding how they functioned in groups. In groups run by trained professionals, children could freely give and take, learn and benefit from mutuality, and express their feelings about race, religion, difficult situations in their lives, or other topics. Groups were based on the inherent dignity and value of each member and could provide opportunities for youth to experience greater freedom as they learned greater self-control and responsibility.

In addition to this work, Gisa thrived in areas where her professional and personal lives interpenetrated and she could make meaningful differences in the well being of others. Beginning in 1950, under the auspices of the U.S. State Department, High Commissioner to Germany, Gisa made several extended trips to Germany to consult on reconstructing services for youth. Gisa provided training in social group work and the humane, democratic treatment of youth to directors and leaders working with the young. For decades, Gisa received thanks from those she taught both because of the content, and because she accepted the people she taught without question, despite her own experiences in Germany.

Gisa and Paul had another separation in 1954 when Gisa received a sabbatical and spent a year in New York City working on her doctorate in social work at the New York School of Social Work (later, Columbia University). Gisa had hoped to study with Eduard Lindeman, but he died before she arrived, so she studied his works. Her dissertation became a book, *Eduard Lindeman and Social Work Philosophy* (1958). Lindeman believed that social work should be grounded in philosophy and social ethics centered on understanding humans rather than focused on intervention techniques. Gisa maintained this approach throughout the rest of her life. To minimize her time away, this was another period of extremely long days and hard work that Gisa would later refer to as an example of "what one can accomplish."

Gisa was extremely productive and acknowledged in wide circles over the next period in her life. Gisa became known beyond social work as an expert on youth and adolescence, including delinquency, and she served on many local, regional, and national councils. She lectured and taught around the world (for example, in Brazil, Cyprus, Israel, India, Japan, Netherlands, and Thailand), and she entertained visiting international scholars and practitioners. She wrote two of her most important and widely translated books (*Social Group Work: A Helping Process*, 1963; *Adolescent Girl in Conflict*, 1966) in this time period.

At the University of Minnesota she began to work in interdisciplinary and community programs in 1968. The next year, she became a liaison between the central administration and protesting student leaders during tumultuous Vietnam war protests. Gisa felt that her ability to be an effective mediator was enhanced because of her own background as a youth in the anti-Nazi resistance movement.

Gisa's final and possibly most enjoyable position, beginning in 1970, was as director of the Center for Youth Development and Research. In this role, she directed funded qualitative research that involved face-to-face interviews with young girls around the country, some of whom were in delinquency institutions. One project resulted in the book, *Young Girls: A Portrait of Adolescence* (1976). Years later, Gisa recalled that the finding of greatest importance was that girls wanted to be considered as human beings — as individuals — to be treated with respect and to have their voices heard. The Center also sponsored seminars and training for youth workers, developed community involvement projects for youth, and began investigating best practices that provided a basic commitment to justice with compassion — justice with a heart — especially for those least able to speak for themselves. These themes engaged Gisa for the rest of her life and are still part of the mission of the Konopka Institute that was founded in her name in 1998 and works to translate Gisa's values into "direct action that improves the lives of young people."

Gisa was acknowledged with more than forty awards and honors. The two accomplishments that had the most meaning for her reflected her own philosophy and values. First, she was elected president of the American Orthopsychiatric Association (1963), a multidisciplinary organization of mental health professionals concerned with prevention, treatment, and advocacy in the context of social justice. Gisa was among the first women and first social workers to head the group. Then in 1975, Gisa received the highest award for merit from the Federal Republic of Germany for her contributions to rebuilding German social services after World War II. The medal, Gisa said, was "a symbol of my life's struggle against any form of arrogant superiority proclaimed by one group over another."

Paul and Gisa celebrated their thirtieth anniversary in 1971. Paul garnered much recognition when he retired later that year, after which he was able to join Gisa regularly on many speaking engagements and trips. Years later, Gisa commented, "Paul would say: 'I'm happy to come along while you sing for our supper!'" In 1976 Paul died suddenly of a massive heart attack while Gisa was at work. Their almost half-century of mutual interdependence was ended abruptly. Gisa spoke publicly and wrote privately about her personal devastation at the loss of Paul; however, just as she did as a young woman in the face of possible permanent separation, a moment depicted in *Silence Not A Love Story*, Gisa refocused. Following her own "retirement" — or rather her official departure — from the University of Minnesota, the home Paul had reconstructed became her full-time office. Her "calendar" held her many appointments — speaking engagements, near and far; visitors from the past and new acquaintances; new young people; always a cup of coffee, a tray of cookies, and a bowl of candy. Gisa's favorite moments and most peaceful times came from discussions with small groups of compassionate people gathering in front of the fireplace that Paul had built. Gisa always ended by reminding her visitors: "Talk is not enough, we must now DO something!"

In 1985 Gisa gave the annual Konopka Lecture at the University of Minnesota on the occasion of her seventy-fifth birthday. She wrote this talk during a very difficult time when a beloved friend was dying. She said:

"I think that human development is a *continuous* struggle with an acceptance of oneself and acceptance of others, a continuous searching for this real meaning of this strange conscious life; a *continuous* struggle with one's desires and needs and those of others."

Gisa went on to urge her audience:

To accept life with its joys and sorrows;

To increase our capacity to understand human beings, by looking into ourselves, knowing a large variety of people and cultures, literature, and the arts;

To transcend the tragic feeling that it is always "they" and "us," which is the curse of humanity, leading to wars, racism, and all kinds of cruel suppression;

To admit our mistakes and acknowledge others can make mistakes, too.

Gisa did not want to be seen as a Pollyanna. In an interview a few years later she said: "I am not a cheap optimist who denies the dark side of reality. My philosophy comes from knowing pain, feeling hurt, having experienced ugliness, anger and hate, and admitting that they are part of life. It also comes from having seen beauty and kindness." She concluded: "My obligation is to help young people develop, to encourage in them a strength to slay the dragon of despair, to scale hard walls, and yet to feel the warm glow of love."

In May 1995, Gisa was invited by the Berlin government to return as part of the fiftieth anniversary of VE Day. Gisa, at eighty-five went to Berlin for the first time in forty years and I accompanied her. When Gisa was last in Berlin in the 1950s to consult on rebuilding social and child welfare services, Berlin was, in her words, "a heap of rubble." In addition, Gisa's memories of her own childhood in Berlin tended to be grim. She was ambivalent about the feelings that might emerge from the trip and realistically concerned about the physical demands of travel and the extensive schedule of activities. Nonetheless, we headed to Berlin.

I can best describe this with a brief collage of memories: Tears flowing down Gisa's cheeks as she watched little German children welcome us with "*Ode to Joy*," then sing in Hebrew and dance the hora; A poignant reunion, after sixty years, with a very frail Hanchen from the anti-Nazi resistance, who died shortly after; Standing in the doorway of the Cecelia Schulen, her grade school and the only building in her childhood neighborhood that remained standing. Gisa clearly came to a visible and more complete reconnection with her past, something that she appreciated for the rest of her life.

Gisa's life transcended convenient categories. Yes, she was German, but her parents were Polish; yes, she was born a Jew, but Paul was born a Christian. She was well known for her books on adolescent girls, but she was also thought of as "the mother of delinquents," mainly boys. Gisa was a social worker, but her influence and audience included diverse disciplines, ages, and backgrounds. She frequently experienced doubt and sometimes despair, even as she inspired hope in those she touched. Until the end of her life, she continued to believe that good things can come with courage and hard work. While acknowledging differences, Gisa preferred to focus on the aspects of humanity that are common to all.

Gisa never stopped questioning whether she had "done enough," whether she had any meaningful impact on the humane treatment of youth, whether she was "useless" when age forced her to limit her external commitments. Gisa did allow herself to experience the acknowledgments that she received surrounding her ninetieth birthday. It was Gisela Konopka Day in Minnesota; the *Minneapolis Star Tribune* had a front-page story ("*Never forget, remember to tell: Honoring a lifetime of vigilance*") and an editorial (*90 years of striving against hate*). The University of Minnesota Board of Regents recognized her contributions to youth, and the Annual Konopka Lecture was followed by dinner and reminiscences attended by hundreds. For Gisa, the highlight was a group of adolescents who performed in her honor.

Gisa's greatest fear about the end of her life was not death, but that she would be "hanging around," no longer herself. As it happened, although she was frail and often in pain, Gisa died on December 9, 2003 after a very brief health episode. For many, it was a palpable loss, and her life was celebrated with Gisa stories and reminders that now, especially, "We must always remember." Gisa's official legacy includes the Paul and Gisela Konopka Chair in Adolescent Health and Development, the Konopka Institute for Best Practices in Adolescent Health at the University of Minnesota Division of General Pediatrics and Adolescent Health, the annual Konopka Lecture, and many scholarships and awards given in her honor.

When she was in her late seventies, Gisa ended an important address with a quote she attributed to George Bernard Shaw:

"I work to be thoroughly used up when I die, for the harder I work, the more I live.... Life is not a "brief candle" to me. It is a sort of splendid torch which I have hold of for a moment, and I want to make it burn as brightly as possible before handing it on to future generations."

Now, an unexpected gift to Gisa and a contribution to her legacy is *Silence Not A Love Story*, which helps to pass on that brightly burning, splendid torch fueled by courage and love.

Marilyn Frost, Ph.D. *is a Professor of Psychology at Saint Mary's University of Minnesota, Winona. For more than ten years, Marilyn served as Graduate Dean for Saint Mary's Schools of Graduate and Professional Programs in Minneapolis and she has received the University's highest awards for outstanding service, as well as teaching excellence. She studies personality and well-being and has written, presented, and consulted on a variety of topics including treatment effectiveness for adolescent sexual offenders, life planning strategies for women, and experiential education. Marilyn cherishes and continues to benefit from the close friendship she shared with Gisa Konopka for more than thirty years.*

Bibliography

About Gisa Konopka

Courage and Love by Gisela Konopka (MN: Beaver's Pond Press, 1997, 1988).

Rebellious Spirit by Janice Andrews-Schenk (MN: Beaver's Pond Press 2005).

About Germany

Before the Deluge: A Portrait of Berlin in the 1920s by Otto Friedrich (NY: Harper Collins Publishers 1995).

Defying Hitler, A Memoir by Sebastian Haffner (NY: Picador; Farrar, Straus and Giroux 2000).

Music While Drowning, German Expressionist Poems, ed. David Miller, Stephen Watts (London: Tate Publishing 2003).

Weimar Culture: The Outsider as Insider by Peter Gay (New York: Harper & Row 1968).

About Resistance and Response

Daring to Resist: Jewish Defiance in the Holocaust, ed Yitzchak Mais, Museum of Jewish Heritage-A Living Memorial to the Holocaust.

Resistance to National Socialism, by Dr. Peter Steinback and Dr. Johannes Tuchel, translated into English by John Grossman (Berlin: German Resistance Memorial Center).

The Diary of a Young Girl by Anne Frank, trans. by B.M. Booyaart (New York: Bantam Books 1967, 1993).

About the Nazis

The Holocaust Chronicle, ed. David J. Hogan (Ill: Publications International Ltd. 2003).

The Rise and Fall of the Third Reich by William L. Shirer (New York: Simon & Schuster 1960).

State of Deception: The Power of Nazi Propaganda by Steven Luckert and Susan Bachrach (DC: United States Holocaust Memorial Museum 2008).

Who Voted for Hitler? by Richard F. Hamilton (Princeton, N.J.: Princeton University Press 1982).

The World Must Know by Michael Berenbaum (DC: United States Holocaust Memorial Museum 1993, 2006).

Websites

German Resistance Memorial Center
http://www.gdw-berlin.de/index-e.php

Adolph Hitler's Rise to Power, Time Magazine
http://www.time.com/time/photogallery/0,29307,1707887,00.html

United States Holocaust Memorial Museum
http://www.ushmm.org

Exhibit on German Propaganda, U.S. Holocaust Memorial Museum
http://www.ushmm.org/propaganda/exhibit.html#/timeline/

Museum of Jewish Heritage-A Living Memorial to the Holocaust
www.mjhnyc.org

The Konopka Institute for Best Practices in Adolescent Health
www.konopka.umn.edu